MW01027793

DK POCKET GENIUS

OCEAN

FACTS AT YOUR FINGERTIPS

DK DELHI
Senior Editor Virien Chopra
Senior Art Editor Vikas Chauhan
Project Art Editor Heena Sharma
Art Editor Tanisha Mandal
Assistant Editor Sukriti Kapoor
Picture Research Co-ordinator Sumita Khatwani
Picture Research Manager Taiyaba Khatoon
Managing Editor Kingshuk Ghoshal
Managing Art Editor Govind Mittal
Senior DTP Designer Neeraj Bhatia
DTP Designer Bimlesh Tiwari
Pre-production Manager Balwant Singh
Production Manager Pankaj Sharma
Jacket Designer Juhi Sheth

DK LONDON
Senior Editor Ankita Awasthi Tröger
Senior Art Editor Laura Gardner Design Studio Ltd
Project Editors Bharti Bedi,
Ben Ffrancon Davies, Priyanka Kharbanda
US Editor Megan Douglass
Managing Editor Christine Stroyan
Managing Art Editor Anna Hall
Senior Production Editor Andy Hilliard
Production Controller Samantha Cross
Jacket Design Development Manager Sophia MTT
Publisher Andrew Macintyre
Associate Publishing Director Liz Wheeler
Art Director Karen Self
Publishing Director Jonathan Metcalf

Author Ben Hubbard
Consultant Derek Harvey

First American Edition, 2021
Published in the United States by DK Publishing
1745 Broadway, 20th Floor, New York, NY 10019

Copyright © 2021 Dorling Kindersley Limited
DK, a Division of Penguin Random House LLC
22 23 24 25 10 9 8 7 6 5
006–322652–Jun/2021

All rights reserved.
Without limiting the rights under the copyright reserved above, no part of
this publication may be reproduced, stored in or introduced into a retrieval
system, or transmitted, in any form, or by any means (electronic,
mechanical, photocopying, recording, or otherwise), without the prior
written permission of the copyright owner.
Published in Great Britain by Dorling Kindersley Limited

A catalog record for this book
is available from the Library of Congress.
ISBN 978-0-7440-3361-8

DK books are available at special discounts when purchased in bulk
for sales promotions, premiums, fund-raising, or educational use.
For details, contact: DK Publishing Special Markets,
1745 Broadway, 20th Floor, New York, NY 10019
SpecialSales@dk.com

Printed and bound in China

For the curious
www.dk.com

MIX
Paper | Supporting
responsible forestry
FSC™ C018179

This book was made with
Forest Stewardship Council™ certified
paper – one small step in DK's
commitment to a sustainable future.
For more information go to
www.dk.com/our-green-pledge

CONTENTS

Scales and sizes

This book contains profiles of ocean creatures with scale drawings to show their size.

6 ft (1.8 m) 6 in (15 cm) 1½ in (4 cm)

6 ft (1.8 m)

8 in (20 cm)

A world of water

Earth is a blue, watery world, with seawater covering more than two-thirds of its surface. Most of this seawater is contained in five vast oceans. Beneath the waves, these oceans teem with life. The ocean environment is vital to our survival on land, yet it remains a mysterious and largely unexplored place.

The blue planet
From space, Earth looks like a green and blue marble covered with ocean water. Water makes Earth a unique planet and the only one we know of that supports life.

Chemical soup
Life on Earth probably began around hydrothermal vents deep on the ocean floor. These vents spew boiling hot water containing dissolved chemicals and minerals that are essential building blocks for life.

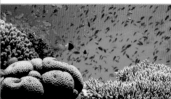

Varied habitats
Oceans and seas make up the largest environment for life on Earth. There are many habitats within this environment, and a vast variety of animal and plant life.

Wild surface

The world's oceans are closely linked to our weather and climate, and therefore have a significant impact on life on land. In turn, human activity on land affects the health of the oceans.

Changing levels

Global warming caused by accelerated climate change is leading to the melting of glaciers and polar ice. This is, in turn, warming the oceans and causing sea levels to rise, threatening low-lying coastal regions and islands with flooding.

Muir Glacier, Alaska, 1941

The extent of this glacier reduced by nearly 7 miles (11 km) between 1941 and 2004.

Muir Glacier, Alaska, 2004

The five oceans

The largest bodies of water on Earth are the five oceans: the Pacific, Atlantic, Indian, Arctic, and Southern oceans. Although the oceans have different names, they are all connected. Together, they make up one large mass of constantly moving water that stretches around the globe.

The Pacific Ocean

Covering more than a third of the Earth's surface, the Pacific is the world's largest ocean. It is also the deepest and contains the Mariana Trench—the world's deepest place. Many island chains are found in the Pacific, including the islands of Hawaii.

The Atlantic Ocean

Around half the size of the Pacific, the Atlantic is the world's second-largest ocean. It separates the continents of Europe and Africa from North and South America.

A rocky outcrop off the coast of Penzance, Cornwall, UK, near the western edge of Europe

The Indian Ocean

Most of the Indian Ocean lies around the Earth's equator. This means it contains mainly warm, tropical water, which can reach 82°F (28°C). Little wonder, then, that it is home to some of the largest coral reefs on Earth. However, the water becomes cooler as it mingles with the Southern Ocean.

Arctic icebergs

The polar oceans

The Northern Hemisphere's Arctic Ocean and the Southern Hemisphere's Southern Ocean are the world's coldest waters. They are fringed with vast ice sheets and feature floating icebergs. Global warming is causing a lot of this ice to melt.

Arctic Ocean

Southern Ocean

Sea and land

Seas are large areas of salty water partly surrounded by land. Some seas, such as the Caspian, are entirely landlocked. Others feed into oceans; the Mediterranean (right), for example, links to the Atlantic Ocean.

How the oceans were formed

The oceans are nearly as old as the Earth itself. They formed four billion years ago as the molten Earth cooled and clouds of condensed water rained onto the surface. Over millions of years, this rainwater flooded the planet and created one global ocean.

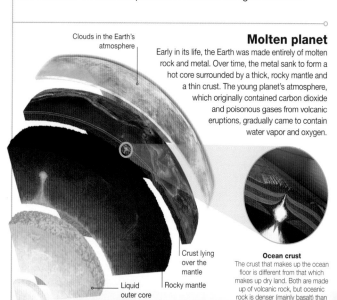

Molten planet

Early in its life, the Earth was made entirely of molten rock and metal. Over time, the metal sank to form a hot core surrounded by a thick, rocky mantle and a thin crust. The young planet's atmosphere, which originally contained carbon dioxide and poisonous gases from volcanic eruptions, gradually came to contain water vapor and oxygen.

Clouds in the Earth's atmosphere

Crust lying over the mantle

Rocky mantle

Liquid outer core

Solid inner core

Ocean crust
The crust that makes up the ocean floor is different from that which makes up dry land. Both are made up of volcanic rock, but oceanic rock is denser (mainly basalt) than continental rock (mainly granite).

Floor formation

The ocean floor is constantly evolving. When forces inside the Earth pull its crust apart, rising molten rock fills in the gaps to form new seafloor. Elsewhere, ocean floor gets pulled back into the Earth to be recycled.

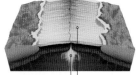

Rising molten rock | Ocean floor forms

Comets

Much of Earth's ocean water came from rainclouds in its atmosphere. More water came from ice-carrying comets that melted as they crashed down onto the planet.

Early oceans

The first ocean covered the globe and no land was visible above its surface. Most of the land emerged as lighter, less dense, continental rock rose to the surface. This land and the ocean around it evolved over 3.8 billion years.

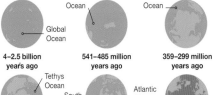

Panthalassic Ocean

Panthalassic Ocean

Global Ocean

4–2.5 billion years ago

541–485 million years ago

359–299 million years ago

Tethys Ocean

South Atlantic Ocean

Atlantic Ocean

201–145 million years ago

66–23 million years ago

Present day

Marine life

Around 3.5 billion years ago, life began as simple organisms in the deep ocean. Over time, more complex life evolved—including giant marine reptiles such as ichthyosaurs, which rivaled the land-dwelling dinosaurs in size.

Fossil of an ichthyosaur

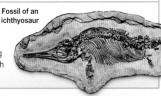

Ocean topography

The seafloor is not a flat, featureless place. Beneath the waves is a vast landscape that rivals anything seen on land. There are towering volcanoes and mountain ranges thousands of miles long. Stretching out below them are hills, plains, and trenches.

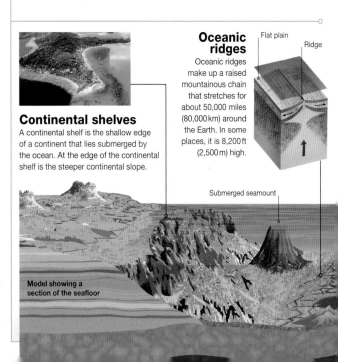

Continental shelves

A continental shelf is the shallow edge of a continent that lies submerged by the ocean. At the edge of the continental shelf is the steeper continental slope.

Oceanic ridges

Oceanic ridges make up a raised mountainous chain that stretches for about 50,000 miles (80,000 km) around the Earth. In some places, it is 8,200 ft (2,500 m) high.

Flat plain

Ridge

Submerged seamount

Model showing a section of the seafloor

Abyssal plains

Abyssal plains are flat, muddy areas of the seafloor. The mud is made up of soft, settled clay or silt mixed with the waste and remains of organisms.

The average depth of the Pacific ocean floor is 14,050 ft (4,280 m).

36,201 ft (11,034 m)

Mariana Trench

Seamounts and volcanic islands

Seamounts are underwater mountains created mainly by extinct volcanoes. Some seamounts rise above the surface to create volcanic islands, such as Hawaii's Mauna Kea.

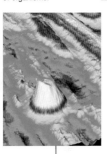

Oceanic trenches

Caused by tectonic activity, oceanic trenches are deep gashes in the seafloor. The deepest trench—Mariana—extends to more than 36,000 ft (11,000 m) below the water's surface.

Oceanic winds and storms

When the sun shines on the Earth's atmosphere, it heats up the air. As this warm air floats upward, cold air rushes in to replace it. This creates wind. Oceanic winds whip up waves, move water around in currents, and create storms.

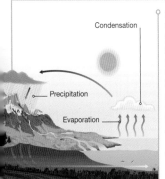

Condensation

Precipitation

Evaporation

The water cycle

Water from the seas and oceans is warmed by the sun and rises into the air as water vapor. As the water vapor cools, it forms rain clouds. Rain falls onto the land and into the rivers, which return the water to the seas and oceans.

Circulation and spin

Warm air rising from the equator moves toward the poles and then circulates back to the tropics. But the spin of the Earth means that, relative to the direction from which they are blowing, winds veer off to the right in the northern hemisphere and to the left in the southern hemisphere.

Rising warm air

Winds veering to the left

Earth's trade winds

Hurricanes

Circulating storm clouds forming over tropical oceans can cause highly destructive storms that bring devastating winds and rain. These are known as hurricanes in the northeast Pacific or north Atlantic, cyclones in the South Pacific and Indian oceans, and typhoons in the northwest Pacific.

Climate change is also contributing to more cyclones. The more heat there is in the sea, the more likely a cyclone is to occur.

Satellite image of Hurricane Matthew over Haiti

Storm clouds

Oceanic winds move in a predictable direction unless they encounter local weather systems. These systems are caused by warm, moist air rising from the ocean or sea. This air carries water vapor, which creates heavy rain and circulating storm clouds.

Direction of the Earth's spin

Winds veering to the right

Air returning to equator

Storm surges

Hurricanes can make the sea rise up and form a large wave of water called a storm surge. When this reaches land, it can cause catastrophic flooding.

Storm surge in Devon, UK

Hurricanes can contain winds of over

75 mph (120 km/h)

and unleash more than 2.4 trillion gallons (9 trillion liters) of rain a day.

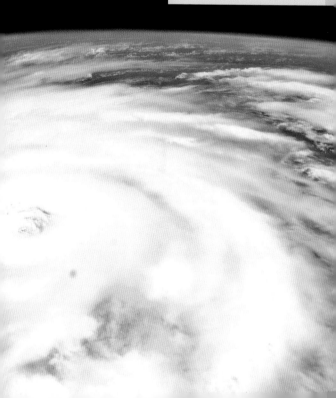

HURRICANES

A hurricane is a swirling mass of cloud and wind that forms over warm oceans and unleashes rain and gales on land with monstrous force. Hurricanes are among the most devastating of natural disasters and are responsible for countless human casualties.

Ocean currents

Winds push on the ocean surface, creating surface currents whose direction is also affected by the Earth's rotation. At the same time, deep in the ocean, unaffected by the wind, there are much slower currents that are driven by changes in the seawater's temperature.

Surface currents

As the Earth rotates, wind blowing between the equator and the poles gets deflected. This sets the ocean's surface currents spinning in circles called gyres—clockwise in the north and counterclockwise in the south. Each gyre has a calm center—such as the weed-choked Sargasso Sea in the North Atlantic.

Free floating seaweed in the Sargasso Sea

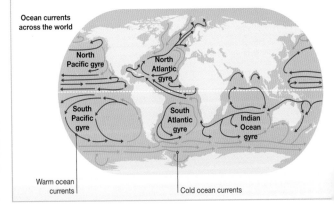

Ocean currents across the world

North Pacific gyre

North Atlantic gyre

South Pacific gyre

South Atlantic gyre

Indian Ocean gyre

Warm ocean currents

Cold ocean currents

Phytoplankton bloom in the Barents Sea

Movement of water

In parts of the ocean, water rises up to the surface from the deep. These upwellings are common near coastlines: water pushed away from the shore by wind gets replaced by nutrient-rich water drawn up from the ocean bottom, nourishing blooms of plankton. The movement of surface water to deeper levels is called downwelling.

Deep-water currents

Deep-water currents help to mix ocean water in a 1,000-year cycle called the global conveyor belt. As water becomes chilled, it gets denser and heavier—so it sinks near the poles. It then flows near the bottom into the Indian and Pacific oceans, where it rises back up.

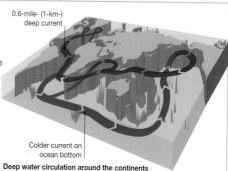

0.6-mile- (1-km-) deep current

Colder current on ocean bottom

Deep water circulation around the continents

Abbey Gardens in the Isles of Scilly

Currents and climate

Currents influence the world's climate by bringing cold and warm waters to different regions—without these currents, many places would be hotter or colder. The Isles of Scilly, off southwest England, lie in the path of a warm North Atlantic current called the Gulf Stream, so have a milder climate than the rest of the UK.

Ocean water

Seawater tastes salty because it contains a lot of salt called sodium chloride, mixed with smaller amounts of other chemicals. It is made up of about 96.5 percent water and 3.5 percent salty chemicals. Oceans turned salty when they were formed billions of years ago, as these chemicals washed into them from the land.

Changing states

Warm liquid water that evaporates changes into a gas called water vapor, which mixes with the air. Freshwater freezes to form solid ice at 32°F (0°C), but seawater freezes only at 28.58°F (-1.9°C). Ice, being less dense than water, floats in it.

Salty water

Water streaming across the land to the sea collects minerals, known as salts. Most of this salt is sodium chloride, which we consume as table salt. This is what makes ocean water undrinkable.

Light and temperature

Light and heat from the sun are absorbed by water, which means that the oceans are brightest and warmest at the surface during the day.

Sound

Sound carries further than light in water, and is four times faster than it is in the air. This enables marine creatures such as whales to communicate across great distances through the water.

Water pressure

Water pressure can be measured in atmospheres (atm). At sea level, the pressure of the atmosphere equals 1 atm. The pressure increases by 1 atm for every 33 ft (10 m) you go down.

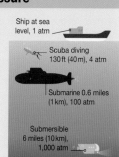

Ship at sea level, 1 atm

Scuba diving 130 ft (40 m), 4 atm

Submarine 0.6 miles (1 km), 100 atm

Submersible 6 miles (10 km), 1,000 atm

Oxygen in water

One molecule of water is made up of two atoms of hydrogen (H) and one atom of oxygen (O). Animals that breathe underwater use oxygen that is dissolved in the water. Oxygen levels are highest near the surface.

Scientists say coral reefs can regrow after appearing to be dead, but only if the water returns to its normal temperature.

Ocean environments

The oceans are made up of four main environments: seashores and the coast, shallow seas, polar waters, and the open ocean. Most ocean creatures live in the shallow seas, but life exists even in deep-sea trenches 7 miles (11 km) below the surface. This is why the ocean is the largest habitat for life on Earth.

Shallow seas
Shallow seas on the continental shelves usually reach no deeper than 655 ft (200 m). Life—including algae, plants, and animals—is abundant here, powered by the sun and nourished by nutrients washed in from land. This habitat has the greatest variety of ocean life.

Seashores
The seashore can be a tough place for ocean life because it is regularly covered and uncovered by the tides. Crashing waves also cause constant erosion, carving out new formations, such as sea stacks, cliffs, and caves.

Polar waters

Covered by thick ice during the long winter months, the Southern and Arctic oceans make up the world's polar waters. Despite their freezing temperatures, these oceans are home to a surprising variety of life.

The open ocean

The open ocean is deep, wide, and mostly unexplored by humans. More people have been to the moon than the deepest spot on the seafloor. In between the surface and the seafloor, the ocean's many layers support a plethora of life.

History of ocean life

The living things that existed in prehistoric times were different from those that are around today. Over billions of years and across countless generations, life changed by a process of evolution. New kinds of life appeared and others went extinct, and the oceans played a big part in the history of life on Earth.

Brachiopod fossil from 300 million years ago

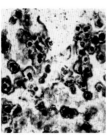

Fossil remains of life forms from 2 billion years ago

Early life

Life began as single cells in the oceans more than 3.5 billion years ago. These evolved into organisms that had more complex multicelled bodies—including animals such as jellyfish and worms—billions of years later.

Early fish

The first vertebrates (animals with spines) were jawless fish, appearing more than 500 million years ago (mya). They evolved into fish with biting jaws, which came to dominate the oceans and included some of the first big ocean predators.

Fossil of the jawless *Cephalaspis lyelli*

Giant reptiles

Life evolving on land included the dinosaurs during the Age of the Reptiles, between 250 and 66 mya. Many reptiles returned to the ocean to evolve into swimming giant reptiles, such as the *Plesiosaurus*.

Plesiosaurus skeleton

Mass extinction

There have been five mass extinctions on Earth. Some of these events destroyed most species of creature that lived in the oceans of the past. The last extinction was around 66 mya that wiped out the giant marine reptiles.

Ammonite fossil

The mass extinction of 66 mya wiped out the dinosaurs, along with 70 percent of all species on the planet.

Modern ocean life

In the last 50 million years, swimming mammals, such as whales, evolved from land-living ancestors. And some prehistoric sharks, such as the megalodon, became giants to prey on them.

Megalodon

Great white shark

Humans and the oceans

Human life on land has always been linked to the oceans. We have used the oceans for travel, trade, and food since before recorded history. Over the last few centuries, however, human activity has started to endanger the oceans. Fortunately, there is growing global awareness that the oceans must be protected.

Overharvesting

We have always relied on the oceans for fish, but overfishing is making many species extinct. Most countries banned whaling after some whale species were driven to the brink of extinction.

Fishing

Whaling

Their fur's incredible insulating properties help keep polar bears warm in the frigid Arctic.

Pollution

Sewage, plastics, oil spills, and chemical run-offs are all poisoning the oceans. However, some countries are now enacting laws to reduce or prevent these forms of pollution.

Oil can kill or harm creatures

Plastic can choke seabirds

Destruction of habitats

Climate change, overfishing, and pollution are putting many marine habitats under severe stress. Some of these habitats are so degraded that their native animal species can no longer live there.

Urbanization of coastlines
As the global population increases, so does coastal development, leading to the destruction of many marine habitats in coastal waters. Some countries are now taking steps to protect these areas.

The loss of their Arctic sea ice habitat due to climate change means polar bears are now endangered.

Seashores and the coast

Situated where the land meets the ocean, coasts are extreme, ever-changing environments. Battered by winds, waves, and weather, and significantly affected by daily tides, they are constantly eroded and altered, with their seashores and rocky cliff faces getting chiseled into new and fascinating forms.

COASTAL CRABS
Brightly colored coastal scavengers, Sally Lightfoot crabs are a common sight on the shores of the Galápagos Islands and South and Central America.

The coast

Coastlines take many different forms—from rocky shores and soft beaches to cliffs, caves, and arches. Between the land and the sea, this is a constantly changing environment.

Rocky shores

Different kinds of rock give shorelines their different characters—such as hard granite, crumbly chalk, or the solidified lumps of volcanic lava of the Giant's Causeway in Northern Ireland (above).

Soft shores

Stone washed away from rocky shores by waves is swept down the coast. It eventually settles as shingle and sand that make up soft shores, such as beaches.

Wave power

Waves pounding the shores grind away at the bases of coastal cliffs and erode them over time. Eventually, the rock at the bottom of the cliff cannot support the weight above it, causing it to collapse.

Sea caves and arches

Sometimes the action of waves carves away at cliffs to create sea caves. If the cave is situated on a headland, the waves can eventually break through the cliff to create rocky archways, such as the Blue Caves of Zakynthos in Greece (left).

Stone to sand

Stones and rocks swept into the water are tossed around by the waves. Over time, the sharp edges are ground away, forming cobbles, pebbles, and sand.

Rocky shores

Most of the life on a rocky shore is adapted to surviving under water, but where the oceans meet the land, resident animals and seaweed must tolerate being left high and dry at each low tide. Those living on the most exposed shores must also withstand powerful, crashing waves.

Living on the rocks

The animals and seaweeds that live higher on a rocky shore spend longer out of water during low tides so need special adaptations to cope with being dry—unless they are protected in tidal pools. Life also needs to cling to rock without being washed away.

Many seaweed species need to stay submerged.

Most seashore animals, such as starfish, can only feed, breathe, and reproduce when under water.

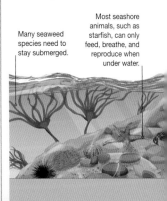

Tides

Caused by the moon's gravity, the tide makes the water rise and fall along the coast every day. At high tide, the shore is completely submerged by seawater. At low tide, the water goes back, leaving the shore dry. The creatures left behind are adapted to living briefly on land.

Tidal pools

Tidal pools keep their water even at low tide. Larger pools contain the richest collections of life, because smaller pools can dry out or overheat in the sun.

Tidal pool life

Some creatures, such as sea anemones, spend their lives in tidal pools attached to the rock. As these pools are always submerged, the creatures can survive at both high and low tide.

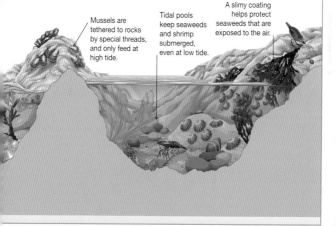

Mussels are tethered to rocks by special threads, and only feed at high tide.

Tidal pools keep seaweeds and shrimp submerged, even at low tide.

A slimy coating helps protect seaweeds that are exposed to the air.

FOCUS ON ...
SEA ANEMONE

Slow-moving predators, sea anemones devour any small prey that strays near their stinging tentacles.

Rocky shore life

Life between the tides includes a huge variety of animals that live attached to the rocks or move between the nooks and crannies, as well as seaweeds that thrive in the sunlight.

Grunt sculpin
Rhamphocottus richardsonii

The bottom-living grunt sculpin uses its fins to crawl over rocks and seaweed, and may take shelter inside the empty shells of giant barnacles. Covered with small plates and spines, this fish has a unique appearance.

RANGE	North Pacific Ocean
SIZE	3½ in (9 cm)
GROUP	Mail-cheeked fish

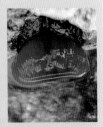

▲ The beadlet anemone retracts its tentacles when exposed at low tide.

▲ When submerged, it extends its tentacles to paralyze and pull its prey into its mouth.

Coralline seaweed
Corallina officinalis

Like other seaweeds, this species is attached to rocks by a sucker-like structure called a holdfast. Its pink, coral-like fronds are common in tidal pools.

RANGE	Atlantic and Pacific oceans
SIZE	4½ in (12 cm)
GROUP	Red seaweed

Rock gunnel
Pholis gunnellus

Often mistaken for an eel, this flat, elongated fish is very slippery, allowing it to easily slip away from predators. Females lay their eggs in shells and crevices.

RANGE	North Atlantic Ocean
SIZE	10 in (25 cm)
GROUP	Mail-cheeked fish

Purple starfish
Pisaster ochraceus

An aggressive but slow-moving hunter, the purple starfish feeds on many animals, including mussels. It grabs the mussel in its arms and pulls the shell apart.

RANGE	Eastern Pacific Ocean
SIZE	14 in (35 cm) arm span
GROUP	Echinoderms

Soft shores

Over time, solid rock gets weathered, or worn away, by waves, wind, and rain into particles of stones and sand. This sediment is then eroded, or washed away, and settles elsewhere as soft shores, such as sandy beaches and mudflats. A lot of life is buried beneath the surface in these places.

Beaches

Some beaches are made up of sand, but others—called shingle beaches—have bigger lumps of rock called pebbles and cobbles. All these particles are moved about by waves and tides, so beaches are constantly reshaped over time.

A sandy beach in Hong Island, Thailand

Estuaries

Estuaries are bodies of water usually found at the ends of rivers, where freshwater mixes with salty seawater. Sediment washed downriver often builds up into extensive mudflats along the banks of estuaries. Beds of shellfish are common in estuaries, as are small fish, shrimp, and crabs.

Estuary near Dundee Beach, Australia

Mudskippers

Mudflats are alive with creatures such as mudskippers that burrow beneath the wet mud. Mudskippers are fish that not only swim but can also climb, walk, and skip on land.

Spotted mudskipper

Mudflats

The tiniest particles of sediment, mixed with bits of dead matter, settle as mud to form mudflats. Mud is sticky and is a better environment for rooting plants and burrowing animals than shifting sand.

Pollution threatens estuary habitats, and may have caused a 20 percent drop in estuary-dependent fish in just 20 years.

Tidal mudflats in South Island, New Zealand

FOCUS ON ...

CHRISTMAS ISLAND RED CRAB

Christmas Island red crabs are famous for their annual mass migration across the island to lay their eggs in the Indian Ocean.

▲ Every year, millions of these crabs emerge from the forest and swarm to the beach.

▲ Once on the beach, the crabs mate. The female later releases her eggs in the coastal waters.

Soft shore life

A beach at low tide can seem barren and lifeless, but beneath the surface are a multitude of creatures. Many burrow into the sand to search for food, while others hide there in wait for high tide.

Mole crab
Emerita talpoida

The mole crab is named for the way it can reverse into its burrow, like a mole. This leaves the antennae on its head sticking out of the sand. It uses them to sense and catch prey on the beach.

RANGE	Western Atlantic Ocean
SIZE	1 in (3 cm)
GROUP	Decapod crustaceans

Pacific razor clam

Siliqua patula

The Pacific razor clam is an expert at burrowing rapidly into the wet sand with its large foot. Once buried, the clam expels a spout of seawater out above the surface.

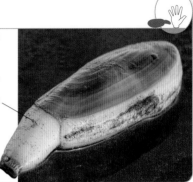

Burrowing foot

RANGE Northeastern Pacific Ocean

SIZE 7 in (18 cm)

GROUP Bivalve mollusks

Lugworm

Arenicola marina

The lugworm lives in deep burrows in tidal flats. It feeds by sucking in small quantities of sand and mud through an inlet hole, filtering out anything edible, and then excreting whatever is left as a sandy cast on the mudflat.

RANGE Northeastern Atlantic Ocean, Mediterranean Sea

SIZE 8 in (20 cm)

GROUP Segmented worms

Sand hopper

Talitrus saltator

Also known as the sand flea, this small crustacean is famous for its jumping ability. It hides beneath the sand during the day and comes out at night to feed on seaweed and other organic debris.

RANGE Northeastern Atlantic Ocean, Mediterranean Sea

SIZE ½ in (1.5 cm)

GROUP Amphipod crustaceans

Ghost crabs can reach speeds of
6 mph
(10 km/h)
while scuttling sideways
across the sand.

Resting in its beach burrow by day, the ghost crab emerges at night to hunt. Its name comes from its pale, sandy color, which allows it to blend into the beaches and dunes until it starts moving. The ghost crab defends its burrow by making loud rasping sounds with its claws and stomach.

Salt marshes and mangroves

Salt marshes and mangroves can be found in places that are sheltered from waves, such as bays and around estuaries. Here, there is a good buildup of mud, which is needed for rooting. While salt marshes occur in estuarine systems across the world, mangroves tend to grow along the fringes of tropical oceans.

Salt marshes

Salt marshes are often made up of winding creeks and muddy pools. At high tide, these fill up with water, while at low tide the plants are left exposed.

Salt-tolerant plants
Glasswort is a hardy species of flowering halophyte—plants that are adapted to and thrive in saltwater.

Mangroves

Mangroves are salt-tolerant trees that are specially adapted to growing in the airless tidal mud. Many grow their roots above the soil where they can absorb oxygen from the air.

A unique habitat
Mangrove forests provide a unique habitat for a variety of creatures, both big and small. One such creature is the archerfish, which hunts by squirting water at prey resting on leaves.

Shorebirds and seabirds

Seabirds and shorebirds are specially adapted for life by the sea. These adaptations include webbed feet, waterproof feathers, and glands to remove salt (from the seawater they swallow when feeding) from their blood. Seabirds spend most of their lives out at sea, but return to shore to lay eggs and raise chicks.

FOCUS ON ...
FEEDING

Shorebirds feed by wading and digging with their beaks. Seabirds dive for their dinner.

▲ Roseate spoonbills have a long beak that flattens into a spoon-shaped tip, helping them dig out prey.

▲ Atlantic puffins dive and pursue their prey underwater by using their wings to propel themselves forward.

Cape gannet
Morus capensis

The Cape gannet can plunge into the ocean to depths of 65 ft (20 m) to catch fish. Although it is a graceful flier, the gannet is famous for its clumsy-looking takeoffs.

RANGE	Western and southern Africa
SIZE	35½ in (90 cm)
GROUP	Cormorants and relatives

Atlantic puffin
Fratercula arctica

The most colorful seabird of the North Atlantic, the puffin has strong wings that help it skim over the ocean and scan for food. It brings back whole fish to its coastal nest.

Bright beak

Small, stubby wings help with swimming

RANGE Eastern North America, Europe, Arctic

SIZE 14 in (36 cm)

GROUP Waders, gulls, and auks

Thick-billed murre
Uria lomvia

A large seabird with a heavy body, the thick-billed murre stands upright when it walks on land. When underwater, it uses its narrow wings to swim after fish.

RANGE Northern North America, northern Eurasia

SIZE 17 in (43 cm)

GROUP Waders, gulls, and auks

Great frigate bird
Fregata minor

The great frigate bird has extra-long wings to expertly glide through the air. It flies high, observing other birds, and then swoops down to steal their catch.

RANGE Tropical islands and oceans

SIZE 3 ft 5 in (1.05 m)

GROUP Cormorants and relatives

Throat sac – only on male birds – inflated as a mating display

Blue-footed booby
Sula nebouxii

The blue-footed booby is a plunge-diver that usually feeds in flocks. When the birds see a shoal of fish, they dive down into the water together to catch them.

Distinctive, blue webbed feet

RANGE Western Central America, Galápagos Islands, northwestern South America

SIZE 33 in (84 cm)

GROUP Cormorants and relatives

Roseate spoonbill
Platalea ajaja

With its pink feathers and distinctive bill, the roseate spoonbill is easy to identify. It feeds by sweeping its partly opened bill from side to side in the water to sift for fish.

Spoon-shaped bill

RANGE Central and South America, Caribbean

SIZE 34 in (87 cm)

GROUP Herons and relatives

Brown pelican
Pelecanus occidentalis

While most pelicans fish at the surface of the water, the brown pelican plunge-dives into the water from great heights, mainly taking Pacific anchovies and sardines.

RANGE North and Central America, Caribbean

SIZE 4 ft 11 in (1.5 m)

GROUP Herons and relatives

Eurasian curlew
Numenius arquata

The Eurasian curlew breeds in inland bogs and moorland, but overwinters on coastal mudflats. Wading in the shallows, it uses its striking curved bill to snap up its prey.

RANGE Europe, Asia, Africa

SIZE 24 in (60 cm)

GROUP Waders, gulls, and auks

Australian pelican
Pelecanus conspicillatus

The Australian pelican has the longest recorded bill of any bird. It mostly feeds by swimming along the water and sweeping its bill just below the surface to trap any fish it can find there.

RANGE Australia, New Guinea

SIZE 6 ft 3 in (1.9 m)

GROUP Herons and relatives

Schools of fish

Fish gather together in large groups called shoals that help them avoid predators. When these groups swim in unison in the same direction, they are called schools. These schools work like a single creature, helping the fish catch smaller creatures and evade capture by larger predators.

FOCUS ON ... SARDINE RUN

Every year, billions of sardines migrate to spawn along Africa's southeast coastline.

▲ The large groups of sardines create a feeding frenzy among predators.

▲ These groups, or shoals, can measure more than 4½ miles (7 km) long and a mile (1.5 km) wide.

Bluestripe snapper
Lutjanus kasmira

It is easy to recognize the bluestripe snapper from its bright yellow color and the four electric-blue stripes running down its sides. A resident of coral reefs and lagoons, this fish schools together around the sandy seabed.

RANGE	Indian and western Pacific oceans, Red Sea
SIZE	16 in (40 cm)
GROUP	Perches and relatives

Yellowback fusilier
Caesio xanthonota

Shoals of yellowback fusiliers often have other fish species mixed in with them. Mainly yellow, the fusilier changes to a red and green color while resting at night.

RANGE Indian Ocean

SIZE 16 in (40 cm)

GROUP Perches and relatives

Atlantic mackerel
Scomber scombrus

Its streamlined, torpedo-shaped body makes the Atlantic mackerel a fast swimmer. Large numbers of the fish school together in summer to feed on plankton and other small fish.

RANGE North Atlantic Ocean, Mediterranean Sea

SIZE 24 in (60 cm)

GROUP Mackerels and relatives

European pilchard
Sardina pilchardus

Also sometimes known as a sardine, the European pilchard spends its life in large shoals and sometimes travels as far as 62 miles (100 km) out to sea to hunt.

RANGE Northeast Atlantic Ocean, Mediterranean Sea

SIZE 12 in (30 cm)

GROUP Herrings and relatives

Shallow seas

Situated on continental shelves, shallow seas are sunlit places that teem with animal and plant life. This life is perfectly adapted to suit every shallow sea habitat—from sandy seabeds and seagrass meadows to kelp forests and coral reefs.

TROPICAL STARFISH
The Panamic cushion star lives in seagrass beds around the Pacific coastlines of Costa Rica and the Galápagos Islands.

Shallow seas

The world's shallow seas lap the edges of the continents and lie above underwater shelves that extend out from the shore before giving way to the deeper open ocean. This is a habitat for several species, and light may penetrate right to the sea bottom, especially if the water is not clouded by sediment.

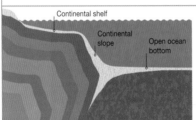

Continental shelf

Continental slope

Open ocean bottom

Continental shelves

Continental shelves can range from 19 miles (30 km) wide to over 620 miles (1,000 km) wide before dropping down along continental slopes to the open ocean bottom. But nowhere are they deeper than 655 ft (200 m).

Rocky seabeds

In some places on the continental shelves, rocky reefs form on the bedrock of the seabed. These habitats are full of nooks and crannies for many different communities of marine life.

Sandy seabeds

Sand created by coastal erosion makes up part of the sediment that covers continental shelf seabeds. This sand is full of burrowing creatures.

Ocean productivity

The waters of shallow seas are fertilized by nutrients running off from land and coming from decaying waste and dead matter. This, combined with energy from the sun, make coastal waters more productive than the open ocean.

Lagoons and bays

Lagoons are shallow bodies of water separated from the sea by coral reefs, barrier islands, and sandbars. A bay is an often crescent-shaped piece of the coast enclosing calm water.

Lagoon in the Bora Bora group of islands in the Pacific

Ha Long Bay, South China Sea

Seagrass meadow life

Seagrasses are the only flowering plants that can survive in seawater. They grow in soft seabeds in warm, shallow water. Meadows of seagrass provide a sheltered habitat for a range of marine creatures, such as seahorses, green turtles, and sea cows.

West Indian Manatee
Trichechus manatus

A member of the sea cow group, the West Indian manatee is a large mammal related to elephants. With no hind limbs, the manatee uses its paddle-shaped tail to propel itself through shallow waters, grazing on plants such as seagrass.

RANGE Southeastern North America, Caribbean, northern South America

SIZE 12 ft 8 in (3.9 m)

GROUP Sirenians

Collisions with boats, entanglement in fishing nets, and habitat loss have left manatees a threatened species.

Green sea turtle
Chelonia mydas

The green sea turtle has no teeth, but a sharp beak with which to graze on seagrass. Although adults of this species eat only plants, young green sea turtles hunt for small animals.

RANGE Tropical and warm temperate oceans

SIZE 4 ft 11 in (1.5 m)

GROUP Reptiles

Spiny seahorse
Hippocampus histrix

The spiny seahorse lives alone or with a mate and anchors itself to seagrass and corals with its tail. It feeds by sucking zooplankton into its mouth.

RANGE Indian and western Pacific oceans

SIZE 6½ in (17 cm)

GROUP Pipefish and seahorses

Queen conch
Strombus gigas

The queen conch sea snail lives on the seafloor. It uses its toothed tongue to feed on seagrass.

RANGE Tropical western Atlantic Ocean, Caribbean

SIZE 12 in (30 cm)

GROUP Gastropod mollusks

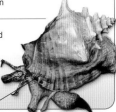

Sand-colored shell

Kelp forest life

Kelp is a giant brown seaweed that grows on rocks in cool, coastal waters. Where it grows thickly, kelp can form whole underwater forests. These forests provide food and shelter for many marine creatures, some of which eat the seaweed and others, each other.

Purple sea urchin
Strongylocentrotus purpuratus

The purple sea urchin is the main enemy of kelp forests. It lives on the seafloor and feeds on the kelp fronds. Over time, herds of urchins can destroy whole kelp forests.

RANGE	Eastern Pacific Ocean
SIZE	3½ in (9 cm) diameter
GROUP	Echinoderms

Spikes for protection from predators

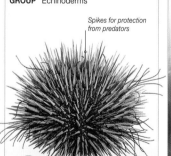

California sea lion
Zalophus californianus

An expert swimmer, the California sea lion has special breathing adaptations for long dives. It is one of two types of mammal that feed on the fish found in kelp forests—the other is the harbor seal.

RANGE	Western North America
SIZE	7 ft 10 in (2.4 m)
GROUP	Pinnipeds

FOCUS ON ...
SEA OTTERS

Sea otters are important inhabitants of kelp forests. They eat purple sea urchins, which are harmful to these seaweed forests.

▲ Sea otters rest by wrapping themselves in kelp and floating on the surface.

▲ After resting, they dive down to collect purple sea urchins, which they eat at the surface.

Senorita fish
Oxyjulis californica

As well as feeding on invertebrates, this fish gains additional nourishment from picking parasites off larger fish. At night, it hides in the sandy seafloor with only its head left exposed.

RANGE	California coastal waters
SIZE	10 in (25 cm)
GROUP	Wrasses and relatives

Mollusks are a large, varied group and each species has its own way of catching and consuming food. Many feed using a tonguelike structure called a radula.

Mollusks

There are more than 90,000 mollusk species, which include octopuses, oysters, squid, and sea snails. Most mollusks have a head, a shell, a soft body, and a muscular foot.

▲ Most squid, such as this Caribbean reef squid, have well-developed eyes for hunting prey.

▲ Sedimentary bivalves, such as this giant clam, filter food from the water with their gills.

Fluted giant clam
Tridacna squamosa

The fluted giant clam has a hard, hinged shell. It attaches itself to hard coral in sunlit waters. Sunlight gives the algae living inside the clam energy to make food, which in turn is shared by the clam.

RANGE	Indian and western Pacific oceans, Red Sea
SIZE	18 in (45 cm)
GROUP	Bivalve mollusks

Flamingo tongue snail
Cyphoma gibbosum

With its soft body wrapped around a hard shell, the flamingo tongue snail is brightly colored to warn off predators. It feeds on the bodies of soft coral, leaving their hard skeletons behind.

Bright warning colors

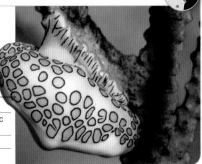

RANGE Tropical western Atlantic Ocean, Caribbean

SIZE 1½ in (3.8 cm)

GROUP Gastropod mollusks

Queen scallop
Aequipecten opercularis

When it is young, the queen scallop shoots out fine threads from its foot onto a nearby rock and stays attached until adulthood, when it releases itself and swims freely.

RANGE Eastern Atlantic Ocean, Mediterranean Sea

SIZE 4½ in (11 cm)

GROUP Bivalve mollusks

Small giant clam
Tridacna maxima

A striking blue, green, or brown color when its shell is open, this clam lives on sandy seabeds and coral reefs, but needs well-lit areas due to its symbiotic relationship with photosynthetic algae.

RANGE Indian and western Pacific oceans

SIZE 17 in (42 cm)

GROUP Bivalve mollusks

Cuttlefish can

change color

in a fraction of a second—for camouflage, to scare away predators, or to attract mates.

CUTTLEFISH
The male Australian giant cuttlefish is famous for the brilliant color changes of his elaborate courtship display. After mating, he protects the female from the rivals gathering around them as she settles beneath his outstretched arms and lays her eggs among the rocks and plants of the seabed.

Bigfin reef squid
Sepioteuthis lessoniana

A large, muscular squid with pear-shaped fins, the bigfin reef squid is found in shallow waters around coral reefs and seagrass meadows. When threatened, it releases a dark cloud of ink to disorient its predator.

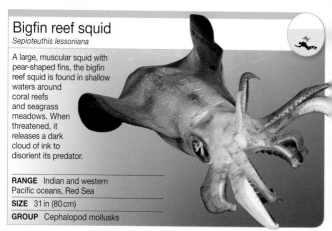

RANGE Indian and western Pacific oceans, Red Sea

SIZE 31 in (80 cm)

GROUP Cephalopod mollusks

Giant Pacific octopus
Enteroctopus dofleini

The giant Pacific octopus is larger and lives longer than any other octopus species. Usually reddish-pink, the octopus can change color to blend into its surroundings and stay hidden from predators.

RANGE North Pacific Ocean

SIZE 9 ft 10 in (3 m)

GROUP Cephalopod mollusks

Greater blue-ringed octopus

Hapalochlaena lunulata

Although only the size of a golf ball, the greater blue-ringed octopus can be deadly if provoked, with an extremely venomous bite that causes paralysis in its prey. The octopus's blue rings act as a warning to its predators by pulsating just before it launches an attack.

A single greater blue-ringed octopus carries enough venom to kill 26 people.

RANGE Tropical western Pacific Ocean

SIZE 4½ in (12 cm)

GROUP Cephalopod mollusks

Coconut octopus

Amphioctopus marginatus

The coconut octopus gets its name from the coconut shells it uses as armor. If threatened, the octopus climbs inside and pulls the coconut shells shut.

RANGE Indian and western Pacific oceans, Red Sea

SIZE 12 in (30 cm)

GROUP Cephalopod mollusks

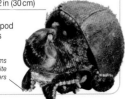

Dark arms with white suckers

Humboldt squid

Dosidicus gigas

The predatory Humboldt squid can chase its prey at a top speed of 15 mph (24 km/h). Like other cephalopods, it can swim forward and backward by squirting water from its siphon organ to create jet propulsion.

RANGE Eastern Pacific Ocean

SIZE 8 ft 2 in (2.5 m)

GROUP Cephalopod mollusks

Crustaceans

Many marine invertebrates (animals without backbones) are arthropods. Most arthropods have jointed legs, segmented bodies, and hard exoskeletons. On land, arthropods are usually insects, but in the ocean most are hard-shelled crustaceans, such as shrimp, crabs, and lobsters.

Harlequin shrimp
Hymenocera picta

A small crustacean, the harlequin shrimp is covered with colorful dots and spots. The shrimp smells out its prey— which includes starfish—with its sensory antennae and attacks with its flat claws.

RANGE Indian and western Pacific oceans

SIZE 2 in (5 cm)

GROUP Decapod crustaceans

American lobster
Homarus americanus

The world's heaviest crustacean, the American lobster has a shrimplike body and ten legs that include two large, strong claws. One claw is used to crush shells; the other has edges like a steak knife that tears the flesh.

RANGE Northwest Atlantic Ocean

SIZE 3 ft 9 in (1.14 m)

GROUP Decapod crustaceans

Ripper claw used to cut

Heavy claw used to crush prey

Giant hermit crab
Petrochirus diogenes

Like other hermit crabs, the giant hermit crab uses a borrowed shell to cover its back, which is otherwise unprotected. When it outgrows the shell, the crab simply looks for a new one.

Shell of a conch sea snail

Giant hermit crabs may be able adapt to warming ocean temperatures, but their metabolism will slow as a result.

RANGE Tropical western Atlantic Ocean

SIZE 12 in (30 cm)

GROUP Decapod crustaceans

Clown mantis shrimp
Odontodactylus scyllarus

A stunning shrimp with a killer strike, the clown mantis shrimp "punches" its prey. It uses the solid clubs under the front of its body to deliver a fast and forceful blow that smashes the exoskeleton of its prey and reveals the soft tissue beneath.

RANGE Indian and western Pacific oceans

SIZE 6½ in (17 cm)

GROUP Stomatopod crustaceans

Echinoderms

Sea cucumbers, sea urchins, starfish, and feather stars are some of the creatures that live along the bottom of shallow seas. They belong to a group of animals called echinoderms, many of whom are shaped like five-pointed stars, have a mouth in the middle, and can regenerate limbs.

FOCUS ON ...
GROWING A NEW BODY

Starfish can sometimes grow an entirely new body from a severed limb.

◄ A starfish loses a limb with vital pieces of the body attached to it.

◄ Cells at the point of the break start growing to create a new body.

◄ Over time, the cells build enough tissue that the limb grows into a new starfish.

Candy-cane sea cucumber
Thelenota rubralineata

This red-striped sea cucumber lives on the sea bottom where it filters sand to search for food. Like all sea cucumbers, it has a fat, fleshy body; a mouth; and tentacles as well as tube feet on the underside for movement.

RANGE	Western Pacific Ocean
SIZE	20 in (50 cm)
GROUP	Echinoderms

Variable bushy feather star
Comaster schlegelii

Up to 200 arms, each lined with branches known as pinnules, help the bushy feather star catch plankton drifting past it. It moves to different locations by floating, crawling, rolling, and even walking.

RANGE Western Pacific Ocean

SIZE 16 in (40 cm) arm span

GROUP Echinoderms

Sunflower starfish
Pycnopodia helianthoides

Although starfish are slow-moving creatures, the sunflower starfish can move at about 4 in (10 cm) per minute. It is also a fearsome hunter, with up to 24 arms that can grab prey.

RANGE Northeastern Pacific Ocean

SIZE 35 in (90 cm) arm span

GROUP Echinoderms

Red knob starfish
Protoreaster linckii

The arms of the red knob starfish are covered with rows of bright red spiny knobs called tubercles. At the end of each arm is an eye capable of seeing light and dark shapes.

RANGE Indian and western Pacific oceans

SIZE 4½ in (12 cm) arm span

GROUP Echinoderms

Fish in shallow seas

Coastal fish are the most abundant in the world, and an amazing variety of species inhabits the shallow waters on continental shelves. Some fish feed on weeds or plankton, while others are hunters of small fish. Some are camouflaged so they can ambush their prey.

Great barracuda
Sphyraena barracuda

Barracudas have pointed jaws and needle-sharp teeth. They attack schools of fish in lightning-fast strikes and use their teeth to tear their prey into bite-size pieces.

RANGE Tropical and warm temperate oceans

SIZE 6 ft 7 in (2 m)

GROUP Barracudas and billfish

Distinctive silver, shining scales

Formidable predators, barracudas are fast movers with a top speed of 36 mph (58 km/h).

Back dorsal fin for acceleration

Marbled stargazer

Uranoscopus bicinctus

This fish has eyes on the top of its head. These help it to spot and launch an attack on unsuspecting prey from its position buried in sand on the seabed.

RANGE Eastern Indian and western Pacific oceans

SIZE 8 in (20 cm)

GROUP Weever fish and relatives

Snowflake eel

Echidna nebulosa

An active nocturnal hunter, the snowflake eel has sharp teeth that can easily cut through flesh and the shells of small crustaceans.

RANGE Indian and Pacific oceans, Red Sea

SIZE 3 ft 3 in (1 m)

GROUP Eels

Red gurnard

Chelidonichthys cuculus

A bottom-dwelling fish that lives on sandy and rocky seabeds, the red gurnard has a spiny fin that acts like a finger to find food.

LOCATION Northeastern Atlantic Ocean, Mediterranean Sea

SIZE 28 in (70 cm)

GROUP Mail-cheeked fish

Spiny food-finding fin

Cartilaginous fish

Shallow seas that are rich with life and teem with shoals of fish provide plenty of food for sharks and rays. These predators have skeletons made from rubbery cartilage—rather than harder, heavier bone—and bodies that are oily, all of which help make them buoyant in the water.

Caribbean reef shark
Carcharhinus perezii

A common sight in tropical waters, the Caribbean reef shark often rests on the seabed, where it uses its throat to pump water over its gills.

Bull shark
Carcharhinus leucas

The bull shark is an aggressive hunter that sometimes also attacks humans. One of the few shark species that can swim in both fresh- and saltwater, it favors murky waters where it can stay hidden.

RANGE Tropical and warm temperate coastlines and rivers

SIZE 11 ft 2 in (3.4 m)

GROUP Sharks

RANGE Caribbean, eastern
South America

SIZE 9 ft 10 in (3 m)

GROUP Sharks

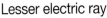

Lesser electric ray
Narcine bancroftii

This slow-moving ray, also known as the
Caribbean numbfish, has up to 26 rows of
sharp teeth and two electric organs that it
uses to fight off predators and stun prey.

RANGE Caribbean

SIZE 26 in (65 cm)

GROUP Skates and rays

Tiger shark
Galeocerdo cuvier

A voracious killer, the tiger
shark is known to fatally attack
humans. Known as the "trash
can of the sea," it eats almost
anything it sees—tires and
license plates have been
among the unusual things
found in the stomachs of
tiger sharks.

Sharp, serrated
teeth for tearing
through prey

RANGE Tropical and warm
temperate oceans

SIZE 24 ft 3 in (7.4 m)

GROUP Sharks

Measuring more than 135,000 sq miles (350,000 sq km), the Great Barrier Reef is

the largest living structure

on Earth. It can even be seen from space.

GREAT BARRIER REEF
Coral reefs, such as the Great Barrier Reef,
are complex, rainbow-colored habitats that
teem with many thousands of different creatures.
Fish, lobsters, clams, seahorses, and sea turtles
are just a few of the resident marine species
that rely on coral reefs for their survival.

Coral reefs

Coral reefs are vast, colorful ecosystems found in clear, shallow tropical waters. Built from the skeletons of coral polyps, the reefs are rocky ridges that support the greatest variety of life in the oceans. These "rainforests of the seas" are at risk, however.

What is coral?

Coral is a colony of thousands of soft animals, called polyps, with tentacles for catching planktonic food. The polyps produce a stony outer skeleton that builds up under them as a solid rocky foundation, which becomes the coral reef.

Open cup coral polyps

Types of coral reef

It takes thousands of years for rocky coral foundations to build up into massive reefs. There are three types of reefs: fringing reefs, barrier reefs, and atolls. Fringing reefs are the most common.

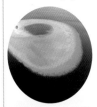

Atolls are reefs around volcanic islands

Fringing reefs grow close to the coast

Barrier reefs are separated from the coast by a channel

Corals at risk

The polyps of many kinds of corals contain tiny algae called zooxanthellae. As well as giving some corals color, these algae help nourish them by photosynthesizing in sunlight. However, global warming is threatening this symbiotic partnership.

Warming water:
Warming water makes polyps spit out their zooxanthellae. This bleaches the coral white (below) and starves it of food, and can eventually make it die.

Overfishing: Overfishing can end up reducing the numbers of algae-eating animals. This allows algae to grow unchecked and smother the reef.

Pollution: Many forms of pollution, including chemical run-offs from factories, oil spills, plastic, and fertilizer from farms, can poison coral reefs in nearby waters.

Acidity: Extra carbon dioxide in oceans causes acidity that prevents corals from building strong skeletons. This leaves them vulnerable to breaking and dying.

Coral reef life

Fueled by sunlight and bathed in warm, tropical waters, coral reefs are crowded with thousands of species, making them the most diverse ocean habitats on the planet. Fish and other animals blaze with different colors as a way of recognizing their own kind—or of warning others to stay away.

FOCUS ON ...
ALGAE IN CORALS

Zooxanthellae are tiny algae that live inside coral polyps.

◀ Zooxanthellae live in the gut lining of the polyp and in surrounding water.

◀ The zooxanthellae in the water have tails that help them swim.

◀ The zooxanthellae inside the polyp are tailless and do not swim.

Christmas tree worm
Spirobranchus giganteus

The Christmas tree worm cements its hard, tubelike body onto a coral reef and uses its feathery tentacles to catch plankton floating in the water.

RANGE	Tropical oceans
SIZE	8 in (20 cm)
GROUP	Segmented worms

Reef squid
Sepioteuthis sepioidea

Fins to help
with propulsion

The reef squid can propel itself
6 ft 7 in (2 m) out of the water and
fly for 32 ft 10 in (10 m) through
the air before reentry.

RANGE Tropical western Atlantic
Ocean, Caribbean

SIZE 16 in (40 cm)

GROUP Cephalopod mollusks

Pygmy seahorse
Hippocampus bargibanti

The miniature
pygmy seahorse
wraps its tail
around soft
coral and
stretches out to
suck tiny plankton
from the water
around it.

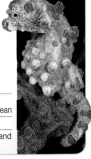

RANGE Tropical
western Pacific Ocean

SIZE 1 in (2.5 cm)

GROUP Pipefish and
seahorses

Day octopus
Octopus cyanea

With the ability to change
colors and camouflage itself,
the day octopus can make
itself virtually invisible to
predators. This means
that, unlike many other
cephalopods, the octopus
feeds during daylight.

RANGE Indian and western
Pacific oceans, Red Sea

SIZE 3 ft 3 in (1 m)

GROUP Cephalopod mollusks

Mandarin fish
Synchiropus splendidus

The Mandarin fish may look bright
and beautiful, but it is covered in a thick,
bad-smelling mucus that helps deter
predators. The fish hunts crustaceans
and invertebrates on the seafloor.

RANGE
Tropical western
Pacific Ocean

SIZE 3 in (7 cm)

GROUP
Dragonets

Butterfly fish
Chelmon rostratus

There are around 115 species of
butterfly fish. This copperband butterfly
fish has a false eye spot, which
may help distract
predators. Its
narrow, pointed
mouth helps it
pluck food from
coral crevices.

RANGE Eastern Indian
and western Pacific oceans

SIZE 8 in (20 cm)

GROUP Perches and relatives

Emperor angelfish
Pomacanthus imperator

As a juvenile, the emperor angelfish
may eat the skin and parasites of
other fish. In adulthood, the angelfish
uses its needle-sharp teeth to eat
small invertebrates, sponges,
and algae.

RANGE Indian and
western Pacific oceans,
Red Sea

SIZE 16 in (40 cm)

GROUP Perches and
relatives

Strong jaws
for chewing

Orange clown fish
Amphiprion percula

Living around coral reefs, the orange clown fish is a sociable species that communicates by making popping and clicking sounds. Clown fish eggs and larvae are cared for by the male parent.

RANGE Tropical western Pacific

SIZE 4 in (11 cm)

GROUP Damselfish and relatives

Fins with black bands

Clown triggerfish
Balistoides conspicillum

The clown triggerfish forages for food around coral reefs. It uses its strong jaws and teeth to crack open hard-shelled sea urchins and crustaceans.

RANGE Indian and western Pacific oceans

SIZE 20 in (50 cm)

GROUP Puffer fish and relatives

Spotted trunkfish
Lactophrys bicaudalis

With its dark spots, triangular body, pointed head, thick lips, and protruding mouth, the spotted trunkfish is a distinctive and easily recognizable fish.

RANGE Caribbean, tropical western Atlantic Ocean

SIZE 19 in (48 cm)

GROUP Puffer fish and relatives

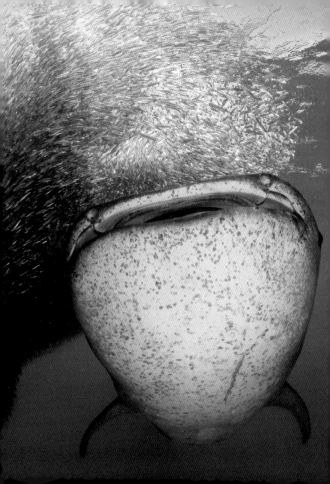

The open ocean

The open ocean is a vast expanse of water that seems to stretch out endlessly to every horizon. Apart from the occasional island, land is often far from view. Below the waves, the water is deep. The deepest point in the ocean, the Mariana Trench, is around 7 miles (11 km) from the surface.

GIANT JELLYFISH
The open ocean is the domain of some of the world's largest jellyfish, such as the lion's mane, which has tentacles up to 120 ft (36.5 m) long.

Ocean waters

On the surface, the open ocean is so vast that the occasional island is often the only land in sight. Below the surface, the water is divided into different depth zones. During the descent to the deep, dark bottom, the temperatures plummet, the pressure increases, and the light fades.

The open ocean

The open ocean contains 99 percent of the world's water. Between the sunlit surface and the darkness of the deep, this is a largely featureless habitat, with islands that rise up from the rocky bottom providing the only isolated specks of land.

Islands: Most islands in the open ocean are the tops of rocky mountains that were pushed up from the ocean bed by volcanic activity.

Open ocean: Most organisms of the open ocean spend their entire lives swimming or floating in mid-water—far away from the solid bottom lying miles beneath them.

Atolls: Coral reefs growing around an island form a ring called an atoll, separated from the central island peak by a calm lagoon.

Depth zones

The ocean is made up of five different depth zones: the sunlit zone, twilight zone, midnight zone, abyssal zone, and hadal zone. The deepest places on Earth are found in the hadal zone.

Sunlit zone: 0–655 ft (0–200 m)

Twilight zone: 655–3,300 ft (200–1,000 m)

Midnight zone: 3,300–13,100 ft (1,000–4,000 m)

Bioluminescent fish

Rocky seafloor

Deep-sea fish

Abyssal zone: 13,100–19,700 ft (4,000–6,000 m)

Hadal zone: 19,700–36,100 ft (6,000–11,000 m)

Oceanic crust

The sunlit zone

Sunlight makes surface seawater bright enough for floating algae to photosynthesize and grow in the open ocean. These produce the food that supports a wealth of animals that drift or swim in this vast habitat, from the tiniest plankton to the biggest predators at the top of the ocean food chain.

Sargassum seaweed

Sargassum natans

Most seaweeds cannot survive in the open ocean because they grow while attached to rocks, but in the calm Sargasso Sea in the North Atlantic, there are thick mats of floating sargassum seaweed, which provide shelter for many animals.

RANGE Western central Atlantic and western Indian oceans

SIZE 26 ft 3 in (8 m)

GROUP Brown seaweed

Single-celled algae

Trillions of microscopic, single-celled algae make up part of the drifting plankton called phytoplankton. Like land plants and seaweeds, they photosynthesize to make food.

RANGE Oceans worldwide

SIZE Microscopic

GROUP Green algae

Copepods

Tiny crustaceans that hang in the water by their long antennae, copepods are part of the group of drifting creatures called zooplankton. Zooplankton feed on phytoplankton.

RANGE Oceans worldwide

SIZE 0.04–0.8 in (1–20 mm)

GROUP Copepod crustaceans

Krill

Krill are tiny, shrimplike creatures that form vast swarms that are fed upon by fish, birds, and mammals. Krill themselves feed on phytoplankton.

RANGE Oceans worldwide

SIZE 0.4–6 in (1–15 cm)

GROUP Euphausid crustaceans

Protozoans

The smallest member of the zooplankton group, protozoans are single-celled, like algae. However, they feed on microscopic living things in the water, rather than making food by photosynthesis.

RANGE Oceans worldwide

SIZE Microscopic

GROUP Protozoans

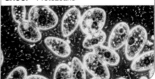

The food chain

All organisms are linked by food chains—energy and nutrients flow from one living thing to another when they feed. On land, plants are the ultimate source of food, but food chains of the open ocean begin instead with microscopic single-celled algae drifting in the surface plankton.

Producers

Single-celled algae in the plankton (phytoplankton) are the producers of the open ocean food chain. This is because they use the sun's energy to produce sugar and other food by photosynthesis.

Cyanobacteria

Scientists have found that human-created microplastics have spread through the deep ocean and entered the food chain.

Primary consumers

Tiny creatures that cannot make their own food feed on phytoplankton. These creatures include zooplankton and the larval stages of some fish.

Krill

Secondary consumers

The smallest carnivores make up the third level of the food chain. They feed on the primary consumers that have already digested their food of phytoplankton.

Tuna

Lantern fish

Tertiary consumers

Secondary consumers are prey for larger hunters called tertiary consumers. An example is tuna, which is then eaten by shark.

Quaternary consumers

The biggest, most powerful predators are at the top of the food chain. Each top predator needs a large expanse of habitat to supply the food that it needs.

Great white shark

Jellyfish

Jellyfish are not fish at all, but soft, jellylike creatures called cnidarians that do not have a heart, brain, bones, or blood. Most jellyfish are armed with long, stinging tentacles to stun their prey and drag them into their mouths. Their umbrella-shaped body pulsates to propel them up through the water.

Lion's mane jellyfish

Cyanea capillata

The lion's mane jellyfish gets its name from its shaggy tentacles that can be up to 120 ft (36.5 m) long and look like a lion's mane. Each tentacle contains stinging cells, which are like small harpoons that spear its prey.

RANGE Arctic, North Atlantic, and North Pacific oceans

SIZE 3 ft 3 in (1 m) diameter

GROUP Cnidarians

Moon jellyfish
Aurelia aurita

With a body shaped like a saucer, the moon jellyfish drifts through the water, trapping small prey in its tentacles wherever it goes.

RANGE
Oceans worldwide

SIZE 12 in (30 cm) diameter

GROUP
Cnidarians

Crowned jellyfish
Cephea cephea

Named after the crown shape that forms its head, the crowned jellyfish is a rhizostome jellyfish: instead of tentacles, it has frilly arms that end in lots of tiny mouths.

RANGE Indian and western Pacific oceans, Red Sea

SIZE 5½ in (14 cm) diameter

GROUP
Cnidarians

Mauve stinger
Pelagia noctiluca

The mauve stinger has many tiny red spots that contain stinging cells, and a reddish color enhanced by its bioluminescent glow. When startled, this jellyfish leaves behind a trail of bioluminescent mucus.

RANGE Atlantic and Pacific oceans, Mediterranean Sea

SIZE 3 in (7 cm) diameter

GROUP Cnidarians

Barrel jellyfish
Rhizostoma pulmo

This jellyfish is large, translucent, and shaped like a mushroom. It can grow to be larger than a person, but its stings are relatively harmless to humans.

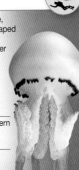

RANGE Northeastern Atlantic Ocean, Mediterranean Sea

SIZE 35 in (90 cm) diameter

GROUP Cnidarians

Predators

The ocean is full of powerful predators that spend their lives prowling the waters hunting for prey. These predators have streamlined bodies and strong muscles that are ideal for fast bursts of attacking speed. They are armed with sharp teeth, gripping tentacles, or slashing bills.

Orca (killer whale)
Orcinus orca

The orca is the biggest member of the dolphin family and the largest hunter of warm-blooded prey. With 4-in- (10-cm-) long teeth, it has been known to hunt prey as large as the great white shark.

RANGE Oceans worldwide

SIZE 32 ft 10 in (10 m)

GROUP Toothed whales and dolphins

Orcas jump, or breach, out of the water perhaps to play or communicate.

Marlin
Makaira nigricans

Swordlike bill

The marlin is a formidably fast hunter, which chases squid and fish. Its long, sharp bill slices through the water to stun its prey, making them easier to catch.

RANGE	Tropical and temperate oceans
SIZE	16 ft 5 in (5 m)
GROUP	Barracudas and billfish

North Atlantic giant squid
Architeuthis dux

One the world's largest invertebrates, the North Atlantic giant squid is a deep-sea dweller that can grow up to 59 ft (18 m) long. The squid's two feeding tentacles can grab prey up to 32 ft 10 in (10 m) away.

Feeding tentacle

RANGE	North Atlantic Ocean
SIZE	59 ft (18 m)
GROUP	Cephalopod mollusks

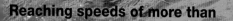

Reaching speeds of more than

19 mph (30 km/h),

sailfish are among the fastest fish in the ocean.

NEED FOR SPEED
A sleek body, powerful muscles, fast reaction times, and a centrally heated brain all help make sailfish the champion swimmers of the open ocean. Their long, sharp bill is used like a cutlass to slash through shoals of smaller fish, tearing them to pieces.

Cartilaginous fish

Cartilaginous fish have skeletons that are made of cartilage rather than bone. The group includes chimeras that have rabbitlike teeth for crunching hard shellfish; flat-bodied rays that live on the bottom or swim in mid-water; and sharks that are sharp-toothed predators or giant, cruising filter-feeders.

FOCUS ON ...
SHARK SENSES

Sharks are equipped with super senses to hunt, kill, and eat their prey.

▲ Barbels are whisker-like, fleshy filaments that detect vibrations made by prey.

▲ Sensitive pores on the snout can pick up a prey's electrical signals.

Great white shark
Carcharodon carcharias

One of the deadliest predators in the ocean, the great white shark is a formidable hunter with large jaws and sawlike teeth. It preys on warm-blooded animals, such as seals, and can even keep its own body at a high temperature, allowing it to chase down prey in chilly seas.

RANGE	Tropical and temperate oceans
SIZE	19 ft 8 in (6 m)
GROUP	Sharks

Common thresher
Alopias vulpinus

The common thresher is an aggressive hunter that usually feeds on schooling fish, often using its tail to stun them. It is a strong swimmer, and one of the few sharks known to jump out of the water.

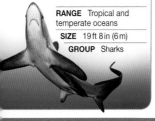

RANGE Tropical and temperate oceans

SIZE 19 ft 8 in (6 m)

GROUP Sharks

Blue shark
Prionace glauca

Highly migratory, the blue shark is known for the long voyages it makes to find food and a mate. Their litters can contain up to a hundred shark pups.

RANGE Tropical and temperate oceans

SIZE 12 ft 6 in (3.8 m)

GROUP Sharks

Oceanic whitetip shark
Carcharhinus longimanus

Fond of swimming through schools of tuna with an open mouth, the oceanic whitetip hunts near the water's surface. It prefers fish and squid but will even eat garbage from boats when hungry.

RANGE Tropical and temperate oceans

SIZE 12 ft 10 in (3.9 m) long

GROUP Sharks

Scalloped hammerhead shark
Sphyrna lewini

One of eight hammerhead shark species, the scalloped hammerhead has a flat, T-shaped head with an eye at each end. The shark hunts by swinging its head from side to side to detect prey.

Hammer-like head, more than a third of the shark's total body length

RANGE Tropical and warm temperate oceans

SIZE 13 ft 9 in (4.2 m)

GROUP Sharks

Pelagic stingray
Pteroplatytrygon violacea

The name of this stingray comes from its preference for a pelagic habitat, which means open ocean. It rarely visits the seafloor and hunts near the surface instead.

RANGE Tropical and temperate oceans

SIZE 4 ft 3 in (1.3 m)

GROUP Skates and rays

Long, venomous tail

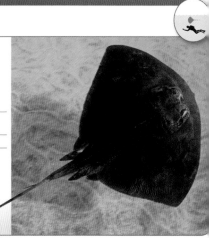

Pacific spookfish
Rhinochimaera pacifica

The Pacific spookfish has a long, spear-shaped snout with small sensory pits that help in locating prey. Once it detects prey, the fish uses its sharp, beaklike mouth to catch and crush its victim.

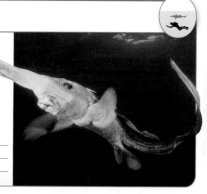

RANGE Pacific Ocean

SIZE 5 ft 7 in (1.7 m)

GROUP Chimeras

Frilled shark
Chlamydoselachus anguineus

This strange-looking shark belongs to a prehistoric group of sharks. Spending much of its time in its deep ocean habitat, it uses its trident-shaped teeth to snag its prey before swallowing it whole.

RANGE Atlantic and Pacific oceans

SIZE 6 ft 7 in (2 m)

GROUP Sharks

Spotted eagle ray
Aetobatus narinari

Unlike most other rays, the spotted eagle ray does not lie motionless on the seafloor. Instead it swims around actively, foraging for food.

RANGE Tropical and warm temperate oceans

SIZE 28 ft 10 in (8.8 m)

GROUP Skates and rays

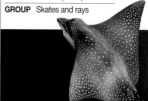

Filter feeders

The largest fish in the world are not fearsome hunters but gentle giants that filter seawater for food. Most of these slow-moving animals use gill rakers that act like sieves, allowing them to filter or strain plankton and small fish from massive mouthfuls of seawater.

FOCUS ON ...
GILL RAKERS
Manta rays and three shark species use gill rakers to filter food; baleen whales use baleen plates to do this.

▲ Basking sharks swim with their mouths open so plankton-rich water flows through their gill rakers.

▲ The gill rakers are like the teeth on a comb, straining seawater out and leaving food behind.

Megamouth shark
Megachasma pelagios

Only discovered in 1976, the megamouth shark feeds near the surface at night, then follows plankton into deeper water during the day. It attracts prey with its bioluminescent mouth tissue.

RANGE	Tropical and warm temperate oceans
SIZE	18 ft (5.5 m)
GROUP	Sharks

Whale shark
Rhincodon typus

The largest living fish, the whale shark has about 300 rows of small teeth, but does not use them to eat; instead, it filters plankton through its gill rakers.

RANGE Tropical and warm temperate oceans

SIZE 68 ft 11 in (21 m)

GROUP Sharks

Giant manta ray
Mobula birostris

The largest ray in the world, the giant manta has massive fins that are 28 ft 10 in (8.8 m) wide. It uses these fins to propel itself through the water while it filters plankton.

RANGE Tropical oceans

SIZE 29 ft 10 in (9.1 m)

GROUP Skates and rays

Tail without the stinger of other rays

Basking shark
Cetorhinus maximus

The basking shark may look scary but is harmless. It swims near the surface, where it filters 2–3 million pints (1–1.5 million liters) of seawater every hour while feeding.

RANGE Atlantic and Pacific oceans

SIZE 32 ft 10 in (10 m)

GROUP Sharks

Cetaceans

Whales, porpoises, and dolphins all belong to a group of aquatic mammals called cetaceans, known as much for their often large size as for their intelligence and complex social behavior. Of this group, whales are the largest creatures on Earth and inhabit every one of its oceans.

Dall's porpoise
Phocoenoides dalli

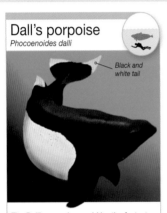

Black and white tail

The Dall's porpoise could be the fastest of all cetaceans, especially in short bursts. It is usually only seen far offshore, but, unlike other porpoises, it rarely jumps clear of the surface.

RANGE North Pacific Ocean

SIZE 2.4 m (7 ft 10 in)

GROUP Toothed whales and dolphins

Sperm whale
Physeter macrocephalus

The sperm whale is the largest toothed whale. Its head accounts for a third of its total body length. Inside the head is the biggest brain of any creature on Earth.

FOCUS ON ...
DIFFERENCES

There are two main groups of whales: baleen whales (Mysticeti), which filter food from water through bristlelike baleen plates, and toothed whales (Odontoceti).

Row of conical teeth

▲ The sperm whale (a toothed whale) eats using the 36–52 cone-shaped teeth it has in its lower jaw.

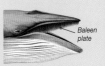

Baleen plate

▲ The Bryde's whale (a baleen whale) eats by pushing seawater through the baleen plates in its mouth.

RANGE	Oceans worldwide
SIZE	63 ft (19.2 m)
GROUP	Toothed whales and dolphins

Striped dolphin
Stenella coeruleoalba

One of the world's most widespread dolphins, the striped dolphin usually lives in groups of about 100 individuals. It can leap up to 19 ft 8 in (6 m) above the water's surface.

RANGE	Tropical and temperate oceans
SIZE	8 ft 6 in (2.6 m)
GROUP	Toothed whales and dolphins

Adult humpbacks communicate using "songs" that can last for more than

30 minutes.

These songs are considered the most complex sound sequences of any animal on Earth.

SEA GIANTS
Growing to 55ft 9in (17m) in length, humpback whales have long heads, jaws covered in knob-like projections, and widely-spaced white throat pleats. These whales spend the summer in cold waters, before migrating to warmer waters to give birth to their calves.

Bryde's whale
Balaenoptera edeni

The Bryde's whale has a large head, which makes up a quarter of its body. Like all baleen whales, it has dozens of throat pleats that expand to hold a large volume of water while it is feeding. This whale eats up to 1,450 lb (658 kg) of food every day.

RANGE Tropical and warm temperate oceans

SIZE 47 ft 7 in (14.5 m)

GROUP Baleen whales

North Atlantic right whale
Eubalaena glacialis

The North Atlantic right whale has raised patches of skin on its head, called callosities. Each whale has a unique pattern of callosities, making it possible to identify different individuals.

Dark, mottled black coloring

Broad, paddle-shaped flippers

RANGE North Atlantic Ocean

SIZE 54 ft 2 in (16.5 m)

GROUP Baleen whales

Humpback whale

Megaptera novaeangliae

Humpback whales are well known not just for communicating with complex songs (which can be heard underwater from 20 miles/32 km away), but also for their group behavior: they work together to blow bubbles that scare fish into denser shoals, making them easier to swallow.

RANGE	Oceans worldwide
SIZE	55 ft 9 in (17 m)
GROUP	Baleen whales

Throat pleats

Large pectoral flipper

Depleted by 20th-century whaling, whale numbers are slowly recovering, partly due to the 1986 whaling moratorium.

Minke whale
Balaenoptera acutorostrata

The minke is the smallest of the baleen whales, which have flat, hanging baleen plates in place of teeth. The minke whale has a torpedo shape for deep dives.

RANGE	Oceans worldwide
SIZE	28ft 10in (8.8m)
GROUP	Baleen whales

Fin whale
Balaenoptera physalus

The second-largest whale in the ocean, the fin whale has a distinctive black or brownish gray color on its back and sides, and white on its underside.

Fin whales are nicknamed "razorbacks" after the distinct ridge behind their dorsal fin.

Illustration of a fin whale

Blue whale

Balaenoptera musculus

Large tail called a fluke

Flippers for steering

The world's largest creature, the blue whale devours many tons of krill during the summer months. It migrates to warmer oceans in the winter.

RANGE	Oceans worldwide
SIZE	106 ft 7 in (32.6 m)
GROUP	Baleen whales

RANGE	Oceans worldwide
SIZE	88 ft 7 in (27 m)
GROUP	Baleen whales

Wide tail with a notch in the middle

Sei whale

Balaenoptera borealis

One of the world's fastest whales, sei whales have sleek, streamlined bodies that can reach speeds of up to 34 mph (55 km/h) in short bursts. They usually swim in groups of two to five, except when migrating.

Illustration of a sei whale

RANGE	Oceans worldwide
SIZE	65 ft 7 in (20 m)
GROUP	Baleen whales

FOCUS ON ...
FEEDING

Seabirds have developed several techniques for catching food at sea. These include skimming, plunging, diving, and even "swimming" through the water.

Ocean birds

Seabirds roam far over the open ocean while foraging for food or when migrating. Some, such as albatrosses and shearwaters, spend nearly their whole lives out in the open ocean.

▲ Unusually for birds, many seabirds have a good sense of smell. This is key to the survival of seabirds, such as the albatross, that fly great distances over the open ocean in search of food.

▲ Albatrosses forage for fish and cephalopods by seizing them at the water's surface mid-flight, or very occasionally by making surface plunges or shallow dives.

Arctic tern
Sterna paradisaea

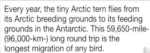

Every year, the tiny Arctic tern flies from its Arctic breeding grounds to its feeding grounds in the Antarctic. This 59,650-mile- (96,000-km-) long round trip is the longest migration of any bird.

RANGE	Worldwide
SIZE	14 in (36 cm)
GROUP	Waders, gulls, and auks

Waved albatross
Phoebastria irrorata

The waved albatross is famous for its courtship dance, which includes head circling, beak snapping, nodding, and waddling. Successful couples mate for life.

RANGE
Galápagos Islands, northwestern South America

SIZE 36½ in (93 cm)

GROUP Tube-nosed swimmers

Sooty tern
Onychoprion fuscatus

Sooty terns are fast fliers that can reach speeds of 25 mph (40 km/h). They fly to land to breed and form colonies of more than 1 million birds.

RANGE Tropical coastlines and oceans

SIZE 17½ in (45 cm)

GROUP Waders, gulls, and auks

Great shearwater
Ardenna gravis

Great shearwaters spend most of their lives flying and are famous for their shrill screams. They use these calls to search for their mates when returning to their nesting burrows after nightfall.

Dark, hooked bill, useful for digging burrows for nesting

RANGE Atlantic Ocean and islands

SIZE 20 in (51 cm)

GROUP Tube-nosed swimmers

The twilight zone

The twilight zone begins around 655 ft (200 m) below the surface. Although there isn't enough light for photosynthesizing algae at these depths, there's just enough for vision, and many animals have evolved large eyes to be able to see. Others make their own light, a process called bioluminescence.

Giant red shrimp

Aristaeomorpha foliacea

The giant red shrimp is commonly found in tropical oceans around the world. It lives on the muddy ocean bottom and feeds by scavenging on scraps left behind by larger carnivores.

RANGE	Tropical and temperate oceans
SIZE	2½ in (6 cm)
GROUP	Decapod crustaceans

Vibrant red color from pigments in the shrimp's exoskeleton

Sloane's viperfish

Chauliodus sloani

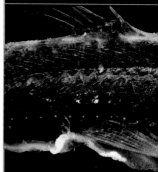

Armed with huge jaws and fang-like teeth, Sloane's viperfish is a fearsome-looking predator. Its long teeth trap prey, preventing it from reversing out of the fish's mouth.

RANGE	Tropical and temperate oceans
SIZE	14 in (35 cm)
GROUP	Dragonfish and allies

Günther's lantern fish
Lepidophanes guentheri

Günther's lantern fish is a small twilight-zone dweller with a unique pattern of light-emitting organs, called photophores, set along its length.

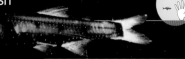

RANGE Atlantic Ocean

SIZE 3 in (8 cm)

GROUP Lantern fish

Large jaws that can be unhinged to grab prey

Giant hatchetfish
Argyropelecus gigas

The giant hatchetfish gets its name from the bladelike shape of its body. It has eyes on the top of its head that help it see prey swimming above it in the faint sunlight.

RANGE Tropical and temperate oceans

SIZE 4½ in (12 cm)

GROUP Dragonfish and allies

Light-emitting photophores

The midnight zone

Starting at 3,300 ft (1,000 m) below the surface, the midnight zone is pitch-dark. Food is scarce here: animals either scavenge on dead matter sinking down from above, or have enormous jaws or expandable guts (or both) to catch and digest large prey that they infrequently encounter.

Deep-sea angler
Bufoceratias wedli

The most distinctive feature of the deep-sea angler is a bit of dorsal spine extending from its head like a fishing pole, giving the fish its name. Tipped with bioluminescent flesh, this lures prey close enough to be snatched by the angler's long, curved teeth.

RANGE Atlantic Ocean

SIZE 10 in (25 cm)

GROUP Anglerfish

Glowing lure at the end of the rod

Fangtooth
Anoplogaster cornuta

The fangtooth has fearsomely large teeth—the two middle fangs on its lower jaw are so big that they have to slot into sockets on either side of its brain when it closes its mouth. These daggerlike fangs snatch up prey, which the fish swallows whole.

RANGE Tropical and temperate oceans

SIZE 7 in (18 cm)

GROUP Roughies and relatives

Black swallower

Chiasmodon niger

The black swallower has an expandable stomach to feed on fish twice its size. Its jaws can open wide to swallow large fish whole, which sometimes rot before they can be digested.

Sharp teeth pointing backward

Expandable stomach

RANGE North Atlantic Ocean, Caribbean

SIZE 10 in (25 cm)

GROUP Mackerels and relatives

Gulper eel

Eurypharynx pelecanoides

Expandable stomach

The gulper eel is a long, skinny fish with an elastic stomach and a slender tail. Its large mouth helps it scoop up many small prey at once.

RANGE Tropical and temperate oceans

SIZE 3 ft 3 in (1 m)

GROUP Eels

Dumbo octopus

Grimpoteuthis plena

Named after a cartoon elephant, the Atlantic dumbo octopus has large, earlike fins positioned above its eyes that help it swim in mid-water. It also has eight webbed arms.

RANGE Northwestern Atlantic Ocean

SIZE 7½ in (19 cm)

GROUP Cephalopod mollusks

Hydrothermal vents

In some spots in the deep sea, volcanic activity under the ocean floor heats water in the rocks to more than 752°F (400°C) and makes it shoot up through holes called hydrothermal vents. This hot water is rich in minerals, and microbes use them as a source of energy to make food, which supports an entire food chain of animals existing away from the energy of the sun.

Life in the dark

Minerals coming from the vents stick together to make tall chimneylike pipes, and may spew upward as clouds of tiny black particles. Vents like these, called black smokers, support a variety of life around them.

Giant tube worms
Giant worms growing up to 6 ft (1.8 m) long live around the bases of black smokers. The worms use the food produced by microbes living inside their stomachs.

Giant white clams
Giant white clams survive by sucking in mineral-rich water from black smokers to support microbes living in their gills, then use the food produced by the microbes.

Model of hydrothermal vents at the bottom of the sea

White shrimp and crabs
Small shrimp and crabs gather around black smokers to feed on the large communities of microbes living on the rocks. These creatures are often blind or partially sighted.

Deep-sea vent octopus
Some species of dumbo octopus live around black smokers and feed on the creatures there. In 2020, a dumbo octopus was found on the seafloor 22,950 ft (7,000 m) below the surface.

Polar waters

The two polar oceans are the Southern Ocean, which surrounds Antarctica, and the Arctic Ocean at the top of the northern hemisphere. These are the coldest oceans on Earth, and their waters are covered by thick sea ice for six months of the year.

ORCAS
Also known as killer whales, these apex predators are found in the polar oceans. Highly social, orcas live in complex family groups led by breeding females.

Polar oceans

The polar oceans are affected by the seasons like nowhere else on Earth. During the long winter months, the sun disappears and the oceans freeze over. During the short summer months, the ice melts, large icebergs break away, and there is an explosion of new life.

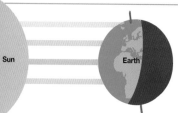

Polar sunshine

Because of the Earth's tilted axis, the sun does not rise for long during the polar winter. During the polar summer, although the sun shines almost permanently, it is not enough to melt all of the ice.

Sea ice

Sea ice is frozen surface water that floats on liquid water underneath. It includes fast ice, which is attached to the land, and pack ice, which drifts and is not attached.

Icebergs

Icebergs are chunks of freshwater ice that have broken away from ice shelves or glaciers and are floating in seawater. They come in all shapes and sizes— some are as small as an ice cube, others as big as a country.

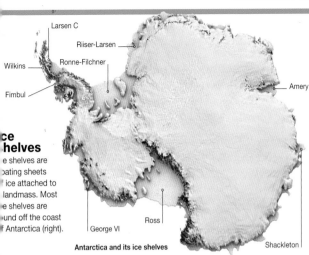

Ice shelves

Ice shelves are floating sheets of ice attached to a landmass. Most ice shelves are found off the coast of Antarctica (right).

Larsen C
Riiser-Larsen
Wilkins
Ronne-Filchner
Fimbul
Amery
Ross
George VI
Shackleton

Antarctica and its ice shelves

Arctic sea ice

The winter ice covering most of the Arctic Ocean melts by more than half every summer. But global warming is making Arctic sea ice melt at a faster speed and in greater quantities than ever before.

Plankton blooms

When nutrient-rich meltwater enters the oceans in springtime, an explosion of plankton occurs. This brings with it a "bloom" visible from space, such as this one in the Arctic Ocean's Chukchi Sea.

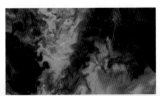

View of a plankton bloom, Chukchi Sea

Polar life

Large ice sheets on the fringes of the Arctic and Southern oceans provide feeding, breeding, and birthing places for seals, walruses, penguins, polar bears, and Arctic foxes. Beneath the ice, a rich supply of algae, fish, and small animals is available to the semiaquatic predators above.

Emperor penguin
Aptenodytes forsteri

The emperor penguin can dive to depths of 2,000 ft (600 m) and stay underwater for up to 20 minutes. In winter, the males stand on the ice to incubate their eggs.

RANGE Antarctica

SIZE 3 ft 9 in (1.15 m)

GROUP Penguins

Leopard seal
Hydrurga leptonyx

A solitary predator, this spotted seal can use its teeth in two ways. When hunting larger prey, such as penguins and seals, the teeth are good for biting. They can also be interlocked to strain out krill from seawater.

RANGE Antarctica

SIZE 11 ft 2 in (3.4 m) long

GROUP Pinnipeds

Arctic fox
Vulpes lagopus

Expert at living in the cold, the Arctic fox can withstand temperatures of -57°F (-49°C). It has fur on its footpads to help it walk on ice.

RANGE Arctic North America, Arctic Eurasia

SIZE 3 ft 7 in (1.1 m)

GROUP Carnivores

Walrus
Odobenus rosmarus

A thick layer of blubber beneath the skin helps the walrus survive the cold. It uses its stiff, facial whiskers to locate food by touch, and is armed with a pair of long tusks.

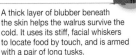

RANGE Arctic Ocean

SIZE 11 ft 6 in (3.5 m)

GROUP Pinnipeds

Polar bear
Ursus maritimus

The polar bear is the largest predator on land. It is protected from the freezing cold by thick fur and a layer of fat under its skin. It also has wide, rough paws that help it walk on ice while it hunts seals.

RANGE Arctic Ocean, northern Canada, Greenland

SIZE 9 ft 6 in (2.9 m)

GROUP Carnivores

Polar bears are strong swimmers. One female swam for nine days without a break in Arctic waters, covering

427 miles (687 km)

in search of floating ice.

LIFE AT THE POLE

Polar bears hunt mainly seals and other prey on land or floating ice, but must brave the chilly polar waters to swim between the floes. A thick layer of fat under the skin traps body heat when submerged, while broad paws work like paddles for propulsion.

Greenland shark

Somniosus microcephalus

This shark prefers to live in the deepest, coldest waters of the ocean. It swims slowly and catches its prey by sneaking up on them instead of chasing them. As well as live prey, it also feeds on dead animals, from whales to reindeer.

RANGE Arctic and North Atlantic oceans

SIZE 23 ft 11 in (7.3 m)

GROUP Sharks

Greenland sharks often have parasites attached to their eyes. This makes them blind over time.

Unusually small dorsal fin

Crabeater seal
Lobodon carcinophagus

Despite its name, the crabeater seal eats mainly krill, which it filters from seawater through sievelike cusps on its teeth. Occasionally it also eats small fish and squid. The crabeater seal is nimble both on the ice and in the water.

RANGE Antarctica

SIZE 7 ft 7 in (2.3 m)

GROUP Pinnipeds

Narwhal
Monodon monoceros

The narwhal is an Arctic whale with a 10-ft- (3-m-) long tusk growing from its upper lip. The function of the tusk is unclear—it may be used in combat or to show dominance.

RANGE Arctic Ocean

SIZE 16 ft 5 in (5 m)

GROUP Toothed whales and dolphins

Blackfin icefish
Chaenocephalus aceratus

While the salt in seawater keeps the oceans liquid even below 32°F (0°C) at the poles, this fish has to rely on the unique antifreeze proteins in its blood to prevent its body from turning into ice.

RANGE Southern Ocean

SIZE 28½ in (72 cm)

GROUP Perches and allies

Humans and the oceans

Humans depend on the oceans for many vital things, including food and transportation. The oceans help regulate our climate on land and provide more than half of our oxygen. But oceans have been under threat due to human activities, and we now understand that protecting them is a major priority.

RECREATION
Oceans can be the focus of leisure activities, including sailing, surfing, and snorkeling. Ocean liners carry thousands of people around the world.

Sailing the oceans

Ever since the dawn of human civilization, people have voyaged across the oceans in canoes, boats, and ships. Advances in maritime technology enabled larger ships to make longer journeys. This opened up the world to trade and exploration.

Phoenician ships

The Phoenicians were great ship builders and traders of the ancient world. From 2500 BCE they set up a vast maritime trading network around the Mediterranean Sea, and were the leading seafaring merchants of their time.

Illustration of a Phoenician trading ship

The age of exploration

From the 15th century, European explorers sailed to different parts of the world aboard great ocean-going ships. In 1522, Ferdinand Magellan began the first circumnavigation of the globe, but died en route, leaving Juan Sebastián Elcano to complete the expedition.

Telescope

Navigation aids

The first sailors mapped the stars to find their way across the oceans. Later, instruments such as sextants improved navigation by measuring the angles between the sun and the horizon.

Marine sextant

Oceanography

Oceanography is the science of the oceans, and includes everything from marine biology and seafloor geology to oceanic storms and seawater composition. Oceanographers often study shallow seabeds, as shown below.

team power

he Industrial Revolution brought steam power to odern ships. This enabled large Atlantic-crossing ers to transport people from Europe to the mericas in the 19th and 20th centuries.

Modern ocean travel

Ocean travel has never been as comfortable an experience as it is today. Modern ships have facilities that were unthinkable in the past, such as hot running water and flushing toilets. Cruise ships provide the service and luxury expected of 5-star hotels.

Explorers

Most of the early ocean explorers had little interest in the waters below their ships and boats. Instead, they were simply crossing the seas in search of promising new lands and potential riches. However, their journeys often led to the opening up of new sea routes and an exploration of the oceans themselves.

Viking explorers

A Scandinavian warrior people who emerged in the 8th century ce, the Vikings used their formidable longships to raid, invade, and trade with lands in Europe and beyond.

COUNTRIES OF ORIGIN Norway, Denmark, Sweden

DATES OF EXPLORATION 793–1066

KNOWN FOR Raiding villages

Maori explorers

Making long journeys across the Pacific Ocean in large canoes, the Maori were the first people to discover New Zealand. They settled there around 1350.

COUNTRY OF ORIGIN Present-day New Zealand, Cook Islands

DATES OF EXPLORATION From 1320

KNOWN FOR Ocean-going canoes known as waka

Zheng He

Using his fleet of more than 300 ships, Chinese admiral Zheng He explored the Indian Ocean and traveled to India, Arabia, and East Africa.

COUNTRY OF ORIGIN China

DATES OF EXPLORATION 1405–33

KNOWN FOR Largest-ever wooden ships

Vasco da Gama

The Portuguese navigator Vasco da Gama established the first direct sea route between Europe and Asia by sailing from Portugal to India.

COUNTRY OF ORIGIN Portugal

DATES OF EXPLORATION 1497–1524

KNOWN FOR Advancing navigation methods

Jacques Cousteau

Cousteau was a French ocean explorer who was made famous by his television documentaries about the undersea environment. He also invented an early underwater breathing apparatus, known today as scuba.

COUNTRY OF ORIGIN France

DATES OF EXPLORATION 1942–97

KNOWN FOR Books and documentaries on ocean conservation

Cousteau in the *Diving saucer* submarine

Deep-sea exploration

Exploration of the underwater world was fairly limited until the invention of the diving suit, which enabled the wearer to stay underwater for extended periods. Submarines now carry people underwater, while submersibles—launched from ships at the surface—take them to even greater depths.

Turtle submarine

Created in 1776 during the American Revolution, the *Turtle* was a wooden, one-person submarine. It was designed to place mines on the English warships blockading New York harbor.

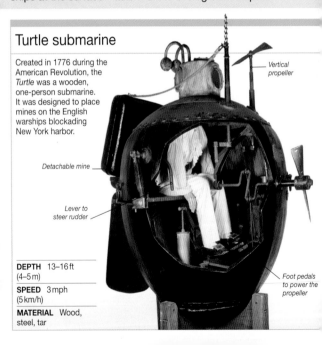

Vertical propeller

Detachable mine

Lever to steer rudder

Foot pedals to power the propeller

DEPTH 13–16 ft (4–5 m)

SPEED 3 mph (5 km/h)

MATERIAL Wood, steel, tar

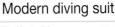

Standard diving dress

Invented in the 19th century, the standard diving dress featured a rubber and canvas bodysuit with a breastplate and helmet made of copper and brass. Oxygen was pumped into the helmet through a long rubber hose.

DEPTH 590 ft (180 m)

SPEED Walking speed

MATERIAL Copper, brass, canvas, rubber, wool, leather

Modern diving suit

The Newtsuit is a modern diving suit with an aluminum shell. This enables the wearer to withstand the pressure at greater depths better than any diving suit before.

DEPTH 2,950 ft (900 m)

SPEED 1.4 mph (2.25 km/h)

MATERIAL Aluminum

Nautile submersible

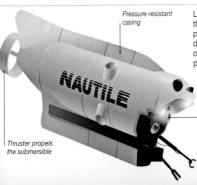

Pressure-resistant casing

Window for viewing

Thruster propels the submersible

Like other modern submersibles, the *Nautile* can withstand the pressures experienced at great depths, including those at the ocean bottom. It can carry three people and is equipped with cameras, lights, and robotic arms to collect samples.

DEPTH To 3½ miles (6 km)

SPEED 1.7 mph (2.8 km/h)

MATERIAL Titanium, buoyancy foam

Modern ships

Humans use modern ships to transport cargo across seas and between continents. Massive tankers and container ships take the largest loads. But ships are not only about transporting goods—ocean travel is also big business, with millions of people vacationing aboard luxury cruise ships every year.

Cruise ship

Cruise ships are large, luxurious floating hotels that carry passengers around the world. The largest cruise ships, such as the *Symphony of the Seas*, have multiple pools, parks, and restaurants alongside thousands of cabins.

SIZE	Up to 1,184 ft (360 m) long
CARRYING CAPACITY	6,680 guests
AVERAGE SPEED	25 mph (41 km/h)

Container ship

Enormous container ships are used to transport heavy loads between continents. The cargo is loaded into rectangular shipping containers, which are then lifted onto the ships.

There is a great environmental cost to shipping: large ships emit pollution and empty their waste into clean seas.

SIZE Up to 400 m (1,300 ft) long

CARRYING CAPACITY 21,413 containers

AVERAGE SPEED 37 km/h (23 mph)

Oil tanker

Oil tankers are huge, ocean-going ships specifically designed for carrying crude oil, which is used to make gasoline. The largest tankers carry enough oil to fill over 16,500 tanker trucks on land.

SIZE Up to 1,500 ft (458 m)

CARRYING CAPACITY Up to 4.2 million barrels of oil

AVERAGE SPEED 23 mph (37 km/h)

Ocean recreation

The oceans are a great playground for people, both above and below the waves. Every year, millions visit the oceans to swim, snorkel, and scuba dive. Others enjoy skimming across the surface on sailing boats and surfboards. Many of these ocean activities, once done only for fun, are now considered sports.

Scuba diving

To explore the depths freely, divers use scuba (self-contained underwater breathing apparatus) equipment. These are air tanks that attach to their backs.

EQUIPMENT Compressed-air tanks connected by a hose to a mouthpiece

POPULAR IN Australia, Belize, Thailand

DEPTH To 165 ft (50 m)

Wind surfing

This is a one-person sport that uses a sail attached to a surfboard to travel across the water. It is now an Olympic sport.

EQUIPMENT Longboard or shortboard, mast, sail

POPULAR IN Brazil, Caribbean, US, New Zealand

DEPTH Surface

Sailing

Sailing is an ancient mode of travel that is today enjoyed by many people for recreation. Craft vary in size, from single-sail dinghies to large, multi-crewed ocean-going ships.

EQUIPMENT Ship or boat, mast, sails, rope, anchor

POPULAR IN Worldwide

DEPTH Surface

Snorkeling

Snorkeler holding his breath to dive below the surface for short periods

Snorkeling is an easy way of exploring shallow waters by wearing flippers, a face mask, and a snorkel—a long breathing tube that sticks out above the surface of the water. Snorkelers breathe though the tube as they swim face down in the water.

EQUIPMENT Feet flippers, mask, snorkel

POPULAR IN Worldwide

DEPTH Surface

Littered across the
seafloor are more than

3 million

shipwrecks, sunk
over thousands
of years.

REMAINS AT SEA

The *Aida* was an Egyptian ship that survived a
German air attack during World War II. However, in
1957 it crashed into rocks when it met heavy weather
while delivering supplies. The *Aida* remains where she
sank in the Red Sea, near Brothers Islands, Egypt.

Food from the oceans

Humans have always relied on the oceans as a source of food. Traditional fishing methods, including spears, lines, and nets, have given way to modern boats and ships that bring in huge hauls, causing concern about the impact of large fishing trawlers on the ocean's supply of fish.

Traditional methods

Many people still use traditional fishing methods to catch enough fish for themselves and their families. These commonly include baited lines, hand spears, and simple nets spread out in shallow, coastal waters.

LOCATION Shoreline

TARGET FISH Coastal species

EQUIPMENT Fishing lines, spears, nets

Traditional fishing tends to be more sustainable: smaller hauls mean enough fish are left in the oceans to breed.

Fish farms

Fish such as salmon, tuna, and cod can be farmed for food in large cages that are submerged in shallow coastal waters. The fish have to be fed, just like any other animal on a land farm.

Nets suspended from frames keeping the fish enclosed

LOCATION Coastal seas

TARGET FISH Salmon, tuna, cod, trout, halibut

EQUIPMENT Cages

Small fishing boats

Small fishing boats that provide fish for their local communities have been around for thousands of years. Today, most are equipped with outboard motors in addition to sails and oars.

LOCATION Coastal seas

TARGET FISH Coastal species

EQUIPMENT Nets, fishing lines, boat

Trawlers

Trawlers drag large, bag-shaped nets through the water to catch fish. While very effective at the job, trawling can damage seabed habitats and coral reefs.

LOCATION Coastal seas, open ocean

TARGET FISH Mid-water or bottom-living species

EQUIPMENT Trawl nets, boat

Energy

The oceans have been a valuable resource for humans for hundreds of years. Oil and gas reserves have been taken from the seabed to fuel the modern industrial world. In recent decades, the world has been turning to cleaner energy sources, such as wind and tidal power.

Tidal energy

As the tides rise and fall, the energy in the moving water can be used to drive underwater turbines to generate electricity. This is clean energy because it does not involve burning fossil fuels such as oil and gas.

ENERGY TYPE	Tidal
DISTRIBUTION	Electrical cables
EQUIPMENT	Turbines, dams, generators

Oil and gas rig

Oil and gas on the seabed were produced from plankton that died millions of years ago. These fossil fuels are extracted by drilling rigs, which sit on seabeds or float on the surface.

ENERGY TYPE	Oil and gas
DISTRIBUTION	Pipeline or tanker
EQUIPMENT	Drill, pipeline, platform, mast

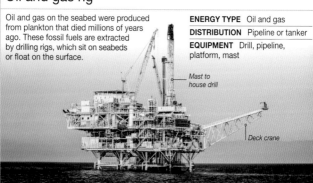

Mast to house drill

Deck crane

Rance Tidal Power Station, France

Long, dam-like barrage catching the water's energy

France and South Korea are among the few countries to harness tidal energy, an environmentally friendly source of power.

Offshore wind farms

Strong sea winds provide a clean source of energy that can be converted to electricity. Wind farms made up of dozens of large turbines harness this energy.

Blades to catch wind

ENERGY TYPE Wind

DISTRIBUTION Undersea cables

EQUIPMENT Turbines and generators

Tower housing cables

FOCUS ON ...
OVERFISHING

Overfishing happens when more fish are caught than can be replaced by breeding, resulting in declining numbers.

▲ Nets used by fishing trawlers can cause damage to the seabed and reefs.

▲ Fishing nets can also accidentally kill creatures such as dolphins, seals, and sea turtles.

▲ Sometimes trawlers can catch an entire school of fish, leaving none behind to breed.

Oceans in peril

Human activities—such as overfishing and pollution—can badly harm the oceans and the organisms that live there. Habitats can take years to recover, and species can be driven to extinction.

Oil spills

Oil is carried around the world on container ships, but accidents can end up spilling this oil into the ocean. Oil floats on the surface and washes ashore, sticking to animals that live there.

CAUSE Damaged oil tankers

HABITAT DAMAGE Pollutes seawater and coastlines

MARINE LIFE AFFECTED Seabirds, seals, penguins

The 1979 *Atlantic Empress* disaster spilled 90 million gallons (340,000 metric tons) of oil into the sea— the world's worst tanker spill.

Plastic

Plastic trash not only gathers on beaches, but also breaks down into tiny particles that get eaten by ocean animals and thereby enter the food chain.

CAUSE Discarded plastic

HABITAT DAMAGE Pollutes seawater and coastlines

MARINE LIFE AFFECTED Ocean food chains, animals trapped in trash

Chemicals in water

Poisonous chemicals enter the ocean from industry, underwater mining, or when pesticides and fertilizers used in agriculture run into the sea from the land.

CAUSE Waste and run-off from industry, agriculture, mining

HABITAT DAMAGE Pollutes seawater

MARINE LIFE AFFECTED Ocean food chains

Warming oceans

Rising levels of carbon dioxide in the atmosphere are causing the global warming of the oceans, which also melts polar ice, making sea levels rise across the world.

CAUSE Rising carbon dioxide levels

HABITAT DAMAGE Flooding coastlines, warmer seawater

MARINE LIFE AFFECTED Corals, coastal life

Saving the oceans

When it comes to the effects of climate change and the health of our oceans, it's easy to feel like we have reached the point of no return. But many groups and people are dedicated to conserving these precious natural ocean environments that are so vital to the future of our life on land.

Stopping pollution

Many conservation groups are trying to stop harmful pollution flowing into the oceans. Some countries have subsequently adopted rules to prevent chemicals and sewage being dumped into their rivers.

Sewage plant for treating waste water before dumping to prevent pollution

Marine reserves

Marine reserves are large areas of ocean that are protected from human interference. They are a safe haven for endangered species and places where animals targeted by fishing can breed and recover.

Protecting coasts

Coastal developments—such as vacation resorts—destroy important habitats such as mudflats and mangrove forests. Some governments are recognizing the harm these developments cause and are taking steps to reduce their numbers.

Cleaning up

The regular cleaning up of beaches helps prevent waste from reentering the marine environment. Many groups organize beach cleaning days for people willing to volunteer their time.

Volunteers cleaning a beach

Sustainable fishing

Fishing is sustainable when the catch is never bigger than the number of babies produced when fish breed. Countries achieve this by having laws that set quotas, which are limits on the number of fish that can be caught. They can also stop methods that harm habitats, such as bottom trawling.

About 10 million tons of bycatch (unintentional catch) is thrown back dead into the ocean every year.

Fascinating facts

MARINE LIFE

- To reach their **maximum height** of around 98 ft (30 m) tall, giant kelp can grow at speeds of 24 in (61 cm) per day.

- Fish living in cold Antarctic waters have a **natural antifreeze** in their blood to keep it flowing and prevent it from freezing.

- Cleaner wrasses are small fish that survive by **feeding on parasites** that live on large fish. They even swim into the mouth of the larger fish to feed on the parasites.

- Many fish can **change from male to female**, or vice versa, during their lifetimes. Other fish have both male and female sex organs.

- The porcupine fish protects itself by quickly taking on water if threatened. The water makes the fish **swell to over twice its normal size**— usually too big for a predator to swallow.

- Parrotfish protect themselves while sleeping by first **excreting a mucus-like substance** from their mouths, which covers them like a cocoon.

- Approximately 50 billion tons of phytoplankton grow in the sunlit zone every year. They also produce **more than half the oxygen** in Earth's atmosphere.

- Most creatures that live on the deep seafloor are scavengers that wait for pieces of food to drift down from above. It can take decades for a **whole whale carcass to be devoured** by these creatures.

- Around **90 percent of life in the ocean** lives in the shallows of the sunlit zone.

- Penguins use their flippers to "fly" underwater at **speeds of up to 25 mph (40 km/h).**

- Billions of creatures make the journey from their hiding place in the twilight and midnight zones to **feed in the sunlit zone at night**. They then return to the deep by the day.

- Green sea turtles can **migrate for more than 1,400 miles (2,250 km)** across the ocean to lay their eggs. Some juveniles have been recorded traveling more than 5,600 miles (9,000 km) across the oceans.

The oldest ocean floor is thought to be more than 200 million years old.

GEOGRAPHY

- The name "Pacific Ocean" comes from the Latin *Tepre Pacificum*, meaning **"peaceful sea."**

More than **90 percent of the planet's volcanic activity** occurs in undersea volcanoes.

Between **10,000 and 50,000 icebergs** form every year in the Arctic Ocean. Icebergs normally have a lifespan of three or four years before they break away and melt.

Waves occur under the ocean's surface at places with different water densities. They can reach **nearly 655 ft (200 m)** in height.

If all the ice in the world melted, **sea levels would rise by 230 ft (70 m)**. That's almost the height of a 26-story building.

According to a 2011 study, more than 91 percent of the total marine species that live in the world's oceans are **yet to be discovered**.

Ocean water absorbs all wavelengths of sunlight. The blue wavelength can penetrate the farthest depths, so **the ocean appears blue**.

More than 90 percent of an iceberg lies hidden, submerged beneath the surface of the water.

The Gulf Stream is a **current of warm water** in the Atlantic Ocean. It moves at 4 mph (6.4 km/h) and influences the climate of places that border the ocean.

RECORD BREAKERS

- The **deepest region in the world's oceans** is the Mariana Trench—its deepest point is about 7 miles (11 km) below the surface. If Mount Everest were placed in the trench, its peak would lie about 1.5 miles (2.5 km) below the surface of the ocean.

- **Earth's longest mountain range**, the mid-ocean ridge, lies deep beneath the world's oceans. It stretches for 40,400 miles (65,000 km) around the globe and about 90 percent of it is underwater.

Some male anglerfish stay attached to the female after they mate. Over time, the male is absorbed into the female's body.

- The Pacific Ocean is home to the **world's largest structure built by living organisms**—the Great Barrier Reef. Measuring around 135,000 sq miles (350,000 sq km), the reef can even be seen from space.

- The bristlemouth fish is thought to be **the most common vertebrate in the world**, with hundreds of trillions to quadrillions living in the oceans.

- Cold water from the Arctic seas sinking to the ocean bottom creates the Denmark Strait cataract, **the largest waterfall on Earth**. It lies beneath the ocean, between Greenland and Iceland. At 11,500 ft (3,505 m) high, it is much taller than the Angel Falls in Venezuela, the highest waterfall on land.

Did you know?

SEAS AND OCEANS

• There are **five oceans** in the world: the Pacific, Atlantic, Indian, Southern, and Arctic.

• Around **70 percent of the planet's surface is covered by oceans**, which hold around 97 percent of all the water on Earth. The other 3 per cent is freshwater: 2 percent stored in glaciers, ice caps, and snowy mountain ranges, and 1 percent stored either in aquifers or bedrock (ground water) or in lakes, rivers, and streams (surface water).

• Sound travels 4.5 times faster through seawater than through air.

• The temperature in the deepest ocean water is between **32°F and 39°F (0°C and 4°C)**.

• The largest ocean on Earth is the Pacific Ocean. It covers an area of about **64 million sq miles (166 million sq km)** and covers around 30 percent of the Earth's surface.

• The amount of **salt in seawater makes it toxic** for humans. A single bath of seawater would contain up to 6 lb (2.8 kg) salt.

• **Less than 5 percent** of the world's oceans have been explored by humans.

• There are **80 seas** in the world.

• The oceans provide the largest habitat for life on Earth; over **94 percent of the world's creatures** are aquatic.

• The South China Sea is the biggest sea in the world. It covers an area of about **1 million sq miles (2.6 million sq km)**.

• The **coldest temperature** of any ocean on Earth, at 28.54°F (-1.92°C), is under polar sea ice.

• The shallow parts of the Persian Gulf in the Indian Ocean have the **warmest surface temperature, at 96°F (35.6°C)**.

• The Dead Sea, situated between Jordan and Israel, is nearly **ten times saltier** than the ocean. This makes swimming in the sea feel more like floating.

• Tsunamis—giant waves tiggered by undersea earthquakes—can travel at **speeds of 500 mph (800 km/h)**.

MARINE LIFE

• **Blue whales are the largest creatures on Earth**, weighing around 3 tons at birth. Babies can drink 25 gallons (100 liters) of milk a day and grow at 11 lb (5 kg) an hour. Blue whales can measure over 98 ft (30 m) long in adulthood.

The **heaviest boned ocean fish**, the ocean sunfish, or *Mola mola*, can weigh up to 2 tons. *Mola* is Latin for "millstone", which the fish is said to resemble due to its rounded body, rough texture, and gray color.

The smallest ocean organisms are bacteria. There can be about **1 billion bacteria in 2 pints (1 liter) of seawater.**

To date, just over **35,700 species of fish** have been recorded in the world. About half live in the sea.

There are more than **one million different types of microbe** in the ocean.

Found in the Atlantic, the 2½-in- (6.35-cm-) long hairy frogfish is **covered in hairlike skin extensions** that look just like fur.

Flying fish can leap 2 m (6 ft) out of the water and fly for 100 m (328 ft) on their outstretched fins.

• The **fastest fish in the world** is the sailfish, which can reach speeds of up to 19 mph (30 km/h).

• The **largest predatory fish** in the world's ocean is the great white shark. It can grow up to 20 ft (6 m) long and weigh up to 1,700 lb (770 kg).

• The six-eyed spookfish is thought to be the **fish with the most eyes**. Two large primary eyes point forward; it has two other pairs of "accessory eyes" that help collect more light.

• Found in the Red Sea and Indo-Pacific region, the puffer fish is considered to be **one of the most poisonous fish in the world.** Less than 0.00014 oz (1–4 mg) of its neurotoxin can be fatal to humans, and there is currently no known antidote.

DEEP-SEA FACTS

The **deeper humans go in the ocean, the more the pressure increases.** If we were to step outside our submersible at the bottom of the deep ocean, this immense pressure would squash us flat!

The **remains of all sea creatures** either get eaten by other creatures or eventually drift all the way down to the seabed where they eventually decompose and combine to form a muddy ooze.

• One of the strangest creatures in the ocean, the Venus' flower basket lives deep on the seafloor and has a **skeleton made from strands of silica, a type of glass.**

• Water deeper than 0.6 miles (1 km) is **completely dark**. The only light comes from luminous animals.

• The **Atlantic hagfish** lives on the deep seafloor and eats by burrowing into the bodies of dead animals and eating its way out through their insides.

Glossary

Alga (algae) A living thing that uses light energy to make food by photosynthesis. Many algae are microscopic and single-celled; others are big seaweeds.

Amphipod A shrimp-like crustacean with seven pairs of limbs, such as sand hoppers.

Antenna A long, thin "feeler" found on the head of some invertebrates.

Baleen whale A whale that has hairy strips called baleen instead of teeth, used to strain small animals from the water.

Bioluminescence The production of light by living things.

Bivalve A mollusk with a hinged shell, such as scallops, clams, and mussels.

Camouflage A color, pattern, or shape that some creatures use to hide themselves.

Carnivore An animal that eats only meat.

Cartilaginous fish A fish with a skeleton made from rubbery cartilage instead of hard bone, such as sharks and rays. Other backboned animals have a bony skeleton.

Cephalopod A mollusk with long arms and tentacles, such as squid, octopuses, and cuttlefish.

Cetacean A swimming mammal with flippers that spends all its life in water and breathes air through a blow-hole, including whales and dolphins.

Climate The average weather conditions of a place over many years. Climate change due to global warming is caused by humans burning fossil fuels.

Cnidarian An invertebrate with stinging tentacles, including anemones, jellyfish, and corals.

Continental shelf Part of a continent that is submerged under shallow seas around the edge of the land.

Copepod A small crustacean that darts about in open water and is part of the plankton.

Crust The outer rocky layer of the Earth.

Crustacean An invertebrate with jointed legs and a usually hard, armor-like exoskeleton, such as shrimp and crabs.

Decapod A crustacean with five pairs of limbs (with front ones often shaped as claws), such as crabs and lobsters.

Echinoderm An invertebrate with spiny skin and a usually star-shaped body, such as sea urchins and starfish.

Ecosystem Living things and their physical environment.

Erosion When particles that are worn away (weathered) from rock get carried away, such as by wind and rain.

Estuary The tidal mouth of a large river, where seawater meets freshwater.

Euphausiid A shrimp-like crustacean, such as krill, that is part of the plankton.

Exoskeleton The hard outer covering of some invertebrates.

Extinct When every member of a species is dead.

Fin A flattened part that sticks out from the body of an underwater animal and helps with swimming. A dorsal fin projects from the back of fish, whales, and dolphins.

Fossil The remains or impression of a once-living thing preserved in rocks.

Gastropod A mollusk with a large creeping foot, such as snails.

Gill rakers The stiff, comblike edges of fish gills, used to help strain food from water.

Glacier A large mass of compressed ice that moves downhill extremely slowly.

Global warming An increase in the Earth's temperatures caused by greenhouses gases trapping the sun's warmth. Greenhouse ases include carbon dioxide, produced by burning fossil fuels.

yre The spiraling pattern of the ocean's surface currents.

abitat A place where a living thing lives.

urricane A severe, potentially destructive tropical storm with winds that can reach over 75 mph (120 km/h).

ydrothermal vent An opening in the seafloor, spewing water heated by volcanic activity.

eberg A large mass of ice that breaks off from the end of a glacier and floats away.

ammal A warm-blooded vertebrate that produces milk to feed young. Most mammals are covered in furry skin, but many aquatic mammals, such as whales, are not.

arine Relating to oceans and seas.

icrobe A tiny living thing that can only be seen through a microscope, including bacteria, many algae, and protozoans.

Migration The regular, usually yearly, journey of an animal to and from different places to feed and breed.

Mollusk An invertebrate with a soft body. Most mollusks, such as snails, have hard shells; others, like octopuses, lack a shell.

Oceanography The study of the seas and the oceans.

Pelagic Relating to the open ocean.

Photophore A part of the body that produces light in bioluminescent animals.

Photosynthesis The way plants and algae use the energy of sunlight to make food from carbon dioxide and water.

Pinniped A swimming mammal with flippers that also moves on land, such as sea lions, seals, and walruses.

Plankton The community of living things that drift with currents in open water. Most plankton are small, such as algae and krill.

Polyp The body of a cnidarian attached to the seabed at one end, with extensible tentacles at the other end, including anemones and tiny coral polyps.

Predator An animal that hunts and eats other animals (its prey).

Protozoan A microscopic, single-celled living thing that usually consumes food.

Radula A mollusk's tongue, usually covered in tiny teeth for scraping food (such as algae) growing on a surface.

Reef A rocky ridge produced by coral, usually growing in shallow, sunlit waters.

Reptile Cold-blooded vertebrate with scaly skin; usually lays hard-shelled eggs on land.

Sirenian (sea cow) A swimming mammal with flippers, including manatees. It spends its life in water but breathes air through its nostrils.

Species A group of living things that share common features and can only breed with each other.

Sponge An invertebrate with a simple, often shape-less, body that feeds by filtering food from surrounding water.

Stomatopod A crustacean, such as a mantis shrimp, with spear- or club-like front limbs used for hunting prey.

Tide The regular rise and fall of the ocean's water caused by the gravitational pull of the moon and sun.

Tube-nosed swimmer A seabird with tubular nostrils that spends much of its time at sea, including albatrosses and shearwaters.

Upwelling When water rises up to the ocean's surface from the deep (often near coastlines). A downwelling is when the ocean's surface water sinks deeper.

Vertebrate An animal with a backbone.

Zooxanthella (zooxanthellae) A microscopic alga that lives inside coral and helps nourish it.

Index

Page numbers in **bold**
show the most information.

Acknowledgments

Dorling Kindersley would like to thank the following people for their help in making the book: Nand Kishor Acharya and Vikram Singh for DTP assistance; Kathkali Banerjee for editorial assistance; Saloni Singh, Priyanka Sharma, and Rakesh Kumar for the jacket; Beth Blackmore for proofreading, and Elizabeth Wise for the index.

The publisher would like to thank the following for their kind permission to reproduce their photographs:

(Key: a-above; b-below/bottom; c-center; f-far; l-left; r-right; t-top, column:row on cover)

123RF.com: Robert McIntyre 80crb. **Alamy Stock Photo:** AfriPics.com 25tc; Kelvin Aitken / VWPics 95ca, 95bl; Amar and Isabelle Guillen - Guillen Photo LLC 44b; Henry Ausloos 35cra; Avalon.red / Stephen Dalton 41tr; Biophoto / Jeffrey Rotman 96crb; Mathieu Foulquie 127cr; Sabena Jane Blackbird 22br; blickwinkel / W. Layer 49cb; Bluegreen Pictures / David Shale 110bl; Justin Chevallier 41b; Helmut Corneli 63br, 64cla; Reinhard Dirscherl 36cb, 60t, 65cra; David Fleetham 54-55bc; Galaxid 111cb; GFC Collection 44t; GL Archive 127cla; Global Warming Images / Ashley Cooper 143br; Granger Historical Picture Archive 129br; The Granger Collection 128bl; Martin Hablautzel 56br; Chris Hellier 129cla; Charles Hood 66rb; Image Professionals GmbH / Holger Leue 139b; imageBROKER / Martin Demmel 38-39.l / Norbert Probst 93ca, 93br,l; Michael Szönyi 72bc / T. Eidenweil 61cra; Michael Weberberger 98-99bc; Juniors Bildarchiv GmbH / Poelzer, W. / juniors@wildlife 85tr; Matt May 53cra; Jens Metschurat 143cla; Jeff Mondragon 52b; Nature Picture Library / Franco Banfi 122 / Sue Daly 87b / Jurgen Freund 36cl / Danny Green 119cra / Nick Hawkins 104t / Alex Mustard 33br / Doug Perrine 102tl / David Shale 109bc / Onne van der Wal 135bl; NG Images 14-15; NOAA 111tr; Michael Patrick O'Neill 63ca; Paulo Oliveira 94tr, 108bl, 110cr, 123crb; Papilio / Steve Jones 118br; Sean Pavone 18bl; Pictorial Press Ltd 129cra; Premaphotos 33cla; Prisma by Dukas Presseagentur GmbH / Gerth Roland 26; Niels Quist 2 141b; RKIve 17tl; Roberto La Rosa 32cl; Science History Images 113tr; Martin Shields 72b; Martin Strmiska 78, 90-91; Samantha Taylor 67tl; Travelscape Images 134bl; Morgan Trimble 85cla; Taxi 113br; Universal Art Archive 126bl, Mike Veitch 61bc; WaterFrame.pbr 77tr; WaterFrame_fba 105t, 142cla; WaterFrame_mus 75b, 89t, 93cra; WaterFrame_tfr 136-137; Stuart Yates 20bc; Solvin Zankl 108-109bc, 109tc. **Dorling Kindersley:** NASA / Arran Lewis

8bl; Natural History Museum, London 28-29bl; Oxford University Museum of Natural History 33cl; Sedgwick Museum of Geology, Cambridge 22cl; Whipple Museum of History of Science, Cambridge 127fl. **Dreamstime.com:** Adfoto 7tr; Agami Photo Agency 106cla, 106clb; Kari Ahlers 31cla; Volkan Akgul 106br; Alimi1968 123bl (water bg); Greg Amptman 32br; John Anderson 74br, 75tl; Anna1311 97bl, 98cl (water bg); Antoine2k 140-141tr; Aquanaut 46br, 47cra; Rafael Ben Ari 80cra; Aurinko 42bl; Rinus Baak 43t; Darren Baker 133cra; Bandit 92bl; Achim Baque 51b; Ana Baron / Aneb 144crb; Tatiana Belova 76cra; Uwe Bergwitz 27cb; Lukas Blazek 67cra; Jaap Bleijenberg 32clb; Darryl Brooks 144bl; Richard Brooks 66b; Jeremy Brown 33bl; Richard Carey 68-69tc; Paul Carpenter 37br; Puntasit Choksawatdikorn 83clc; Deborah Coles 56cl; Brett Critchley 132b; Matt Cuda 42clb; Ethan Daniels 19cla, 73cr; Christian Delbert 139cra; Alexander Demyanenko 6cl; Lian Deng 6br; Digitalbalance 83cra; Yeshaya Dinerstein 56clb; Dirk 45bc; Donyanedomam 107ca; Eckold 102br; Serban Enache 7br; Nick Everett 62bl; Frantic00 131ca; Ggw1962 84cl; Toby Gibson 57cra; Steven Gill 123t; Sophia Granchinho 119cla; Michael Gray 125cb; Myrna Gutierrez 25cra; Christopher Heil 21ti; Hel060808 10cla; Derek Holzapfel 65bc; IshootRAW 50bc; Isselee 62br, 77bc; Luboslav Ivanko 65br; Izanbar 68b, 92clb; 99br; Jocrebbin 43clb; Joyfull 145tr; Oleksandr Kalinichenko 133b; Stig Karlsson 134br; Michele Kemper 31tr; Paul Kennedy 95br; Goetz Kohlberg 116crb; Anatoly Kolodey 116bl; Stanislav Komogorov 142clb, 142bl; Konstik 7cl; Kosmos111 34bl; Irina Kozhemyakina 36br; Lakhesis 51cr; Fabio Lamanna 72bl; Georg Henrik Lehnerer 140b; Puripat Lertpunyaroj 26cl; Harry Liang 145bl; Luckyphotographer 28cr; Gavril Margittai 4bl; Ruslan Minakryn 79cb; Mirecca 76br; Mtlighma 20cl; Nadezdor 107cra; Kim Nelson 37cra; Paul Nguyen 40bl; Noomhh 138b; Siarhei Nosyreu 47bl; Krzysztof Odzionek 85cb; Oksanavg 64br; Boris Pamikov 60bl; Lefteris Papalakis 23t; Parin Parmar 30cl; Lesia Pavlenko 40crb; Sean Pavone 11cr; Peterclark1985 77crb; Planetfelicity 123bl; R. Gino Santa Maria / Shutterfree,LLC / Ginosphotos / Shutterfree,Llc 67ca; Radub85 13cr; Robert Randall 103; Robertlasalle 72cl, 86b; Andrew Roland 17bl; Sarkao 9br; Scanrail 127bl; Seadam 19b, 73bl, 87bc; 87br, 144cla; Seanchon 97cra; Vaclav Sebek 119bl; Vladimir Seliverstov 118bl; Alexander Shapovalov 73tr; Silasfirth 55tc; Slowmotiongli 45cra, 46bl, 88b, 115cb; Smitty411 55cr; Solarseven 9tr; Jens Stolt 37clb; Subsurface 53bl; Taiga 135cra; Tamas 80clb; Tarpan 83bl; Baramee Temboonkiat 21b; Tignogartnahi 87cra; Tupungato 34-35bc, 35br; Sergey Uryadnikov 92br; Valentyn75 20br; Aleksandar Varbenov 29tl; Victortyakht 45bl; Leon Viti 131cra;

Whitepointer 73crb; Wisterias 50crb; Jolanta Wojcicka 2-3c, 51cla; Wonderful Nature 18crb; Wrangel 47crb; Galina Zlatanova 5tl; Zwawol 143cra. Rob Bouwman 139crb **Getty Images:** AFP / Haldor Kolbeins 24bl; Barcroft Media 46clb; Carrie Vonderhaar / Ocean Futures Society 61br; Cartesia / Photodisc 7cra; Corbis Documentary / Patrick J. Endres 114; Cultura / Monty Rakusen 24clb; DE AGOSTIN PICTURE LIBRARY 126cr; DigitalVision / Henrik Sorensen 120-121; Moment / M Swiet Productions 48,/ surangaw 124,/ by wildestanimal 58-59; Moment Open / Brandi Mueller 70-71, / Kerstin Meyer 100-101; Stone / Doug Armand 142br. **Getty Images / iStock:** birdsonline 107br; CoreyFord 23cb; Gerald Corsi 43br; Ray Hems 18cl; kwasny221 29c; Moorefam 13bc; SolStock 25tr. **NASA:** Reto Stöckli, Nazmi El Saleous, and Marit Jentoft-Nilsen, NASA GSFC 4cl; Joshua Stevens 13t. **National Snow and Ice Data Center / NSIDC:** Mónika Bruce F 5b; William Osgood Field 5c. **NOAA:** 4cr; Neil Fisher 55tr; NOAA OKEANOS EXPLORER Program, Our Deepwater Backyard 113cr; NOAA Teacher at Sea Program, NOAA Ship OREGON II / Emilisa Saunders 16cra; OAR / National Undersea Research Program (NURP) 112cr; SEFSC Pascagoula Laboratory/ Collection of Brandi Noble 69tr. **Science Photo Library:** Dr Ken Macdonald 11cla; Michael Patrick O'neill 82b; Sinclair Stammers 22c.

Cover images:

Front: **123RF.com:** Visarute Angkatavanich (dragonet fish), Ten Theeralerttham / rawangtak (Red Gorgonian); **Dorling Kindersley:** Colin Keates / Natural History Museum, London (Mussel Shell), Oxford University Museum of Natural History (Ammonite), Linda Pitkin (Bumphead parrotfish), (Bluestripe snapper), (Parrotfish), Sedgwick Museum of Geology, Cambridge (background), Harry Taylor / Natural History Museum, London (Two krill); **Dreamstime.com:** Corey A. Ford / Coreyford (Blue Marlin), Digitalbalance (jellyfish), Fotofjodor (Main), Isselee (Hermit crab), (Down tingerfish), Kotomiti_okuma (Emperor penguins), Sergey Uryadnikov / Surz01 (Polar Bear); **Photolibrary:** Photodisc / White (Green Sea Turtle). **Getty Images / iStock:** CoreyFord (Megalodon), Choi Ka Kwan (Pygmy seahorse), marrio31 (Butterflyfish); **Photolibrary:** Photodisc / White (Green Sea Turtle).

Spine: **Dreamstime.com:** Fotofjodor.

All other images © Dorling Kindersley

For further information see: www.dkimages.com